Latin America—Diplomacy and Reality

LATIN AMERICA-
DIPLOMACY AND REALITY

ADOLF A. BERLE

Published for the
Council on Foreign Relations

GREENWOOD PRESS, PUBLISHERS
WESTPORT. CONNECTICUT

Library of Congress Cataloging in Publication Data

Berle, Adolf Augustus, 1895-1971.
  Latin America, diplomacy and reality.

    Reprint. Originally published: 1st ed. New
York : Harper & Row, 1962. (Policy books)
  Includes bibliographical references.
    1. Latin America--History--20th century. 2. Com-
munism--Latin America. 3. Latin America--Relations
(general) with the United States. 4. United States--
Relations (general) with Latin America. I. Title.
F1414.B49 1982   327.7308   81-3818
ISBN 0-313-22970-8 (lib. bdg.)   AACR2

This is a reprint of the 1962 First Edition.

Reprinted with the permission of Harper & Row Publishers, Inc.

Reprinted in 1981 by Greenwood Press
A division of Congressional Information Service, Inc.
88 Post Road West, Westport, Connecticut 06881

Printed in the United States of America

10 9 8 7 6 5 4 3 2 1

COUNCIL ON FOREIGN RELATIONS

Policy Books of the
Council on Foreign Relations

With the publication of this volume the Council on Foreign Relations continues its new series of short books on important issues of United States foreign policy. The purpose is twofold: first, to provide readers in this country and elsewhere with analytical studies of the highest quality on problems of world significance; and, second, to contribute to constructive thinking on American policies for the future. These volumes will make a virtue of brevity, not with the aim of oversimplification, but to present with a minimum of factual background and detail the reasoned conclusions of individual authors with first-hand experience and special qualifications to deal with the questions at hand.

The Council was fortunate in persuading Mr. Adolf A. Berle, who has had long and intimate acquaintance with Latin American affairs both privately and in a distinguished public career, to undertake the writing of this book. In the course of its preparation Mr. Berle had the benefit of the views and comments of a small group of Council members which met with him on two occasions to discuss his general approach and conclusions. Responsibility for statements of fact and opinion appearing in the book rests with the author, not with the group or the Council. The Council takes responsibility for the decision to publish it as a contribution to thought on a subject of the greatest moment: the decisions the United States and the Latin American nations must take for the defense of the Western Hemisphere and for a sound and enduring inter-American system.

Foreword

This is an American statement. American writers on Latin American relations rarely describe them with frank realism. Effort is usually made to avoid ruffling the feelings of our neighbors in the hemisphere, and of the American friends of that great region (among whom I am entitled to count myself one) who dream of and work for hemispheric solidarity.

This reticence, I suggest, underestimates the maturity of all groups. Therefore I have here endeavored to write as an American of these problems as they appear in the United States, in the belief that the point of view and necessities of the United States are entitled to as much consideration in Latin America as the needs and viewpoints of the peoples lying south of it are entitled to consideration north of the Rio Grande.

In my view, the nations of this hemisphere, being equals, are entitled to the kind of debate which equals maintain with each other. Too often, I think, the United States' point of view has been withheld; unwarranted accusations have gone without answer, and the vividness of American national interest in the current world problem has not been made evident. I have here written as an American writing primarily for others in the United States, but with admiration for the qualities, the achievements, and the strengths, as well as recognition of the interests, of those other American nations whose hospitality and friendship have been an enduring part of my life.

The phrase, "Latin America," is here used because it is familiar in the United States. There is, of course, no such entity save in a linguistic sense or on a map; and purists use the term "the continent," or "the American states," or the like, because Haiti and the Indian regions are not predominantly Latin. In the United States, nevertheless, "Latin America" has become the historic and popularly recognized term. It seems best to accept rather than struggle against it.

The stream of history constantly moves; a line has to be drawn somewhere, else no book of this kind could ever be brought to an end. Here, for practical purposes, the line was drawn at the close of the Punta del Este Conference on January 31, 1962.

I should like to acknowledge the advice and criticism offered during the formative stages of the book by a small group at the Council on Foreign Relations, including James Phinney Baxter III, John C. Campbell, George S. Franklin, Jr., Walter Howe, Arnold Wolfers, Bryce Wood and Henry M. Wriston. Though the Council sponsors the publication of this volume, the views expressed are my own and no one else should be held responsible.

I am indebted to Mrs. Cynthia Welch and Miss Margaret Poole for typing and assistance and to my friend, John Campbell of the Council on Foreign Relations, who edited the book and steered it to completion.

ADOLF A. BERLE

Columbia University
March 15, 1962

Contents

Latin America—Diplomacy and Reality

Chapter I

The United States
Looks at Its Neighbors

1. THE GREAT CHOICE

In long view, the importance of Latin America far outweighs the disputes, tensions, and difficulties of the current scene. This study must therefore begin by placing the region on a vast chessboard.

In its greatest significance, Latin America may be the principal demographic counterbalance to the rising and somewhat unpredictable power emerging on the Asian mainland. Some students of world affairs have been predicting that the next century—the twenty-first—will be an "Asian" century. They base this conclusion on demographic calculations of the vast populations organized into political blocs or units, of which China and India are the two greatest. Such estimates as a rule leave out the possibilities—perhaps probabilities—of developments in the Western Hemisphere. These possibilities may be summarized and compared with the Asian facts.

Mainland China (including Tibet) has an area of 4.3 million square miles and claims a population of 640 million. One may discount the latter figure, for census-taking is no exact science in China; it may well prove out at less than 600 million when a more accurate count is available, or it could be nearer 700 million. India has an area of about 1.26 million square miles and a population of some 440 million. Close to the two lie a congeries of mainland races and countries covering an area of more than a million and a quarter square miles and with a total population of some 200 million, though none of these smaller countries, or any combination of them or their respective race and language blocs, seems likely to compete with the two Asian giants. Proponents of the Asian theory thus rightly point to a total population of more than a billion and a quarter human beings, polarized into the two power centers—India and mainland China—inhabiting an area (including the interstitial Asian states) of roughly 7 million square miles. "What force," asks this school of thought, "can hope to withstand the awakened power of this growing population whose industrial development is proceeding rapidly, and whose skill and capacity will be at least equal to anything the West can offer?" It is an impressive case.

Yet a glance at the Western Hemisphere suggests that the comparison may not be as staggering as indicated. The United States has a land area of 3.6 million square miles and its present population is about 185 million. The Latin American region has a total land area of about 7.8 million square miles (slightly more than the Asian area we have been discussing) and a total population of about 200 million. If the United States, Canada, and Latin America are added together, the total land area is nearly 6 million square miles (although much of Canada and Alaska, of course, is uninhabitable or only very marginal) and the total population a little more than 400 million. This is a total order of population magnitude approximating that of India, and roughly one-third of the combined Asian population blocs.

Two facts more nearly weight the scales in this comparison. The Latin American population is growing more rapidly (as far as we can tell) than any population bloc in the world. By the turn of the century it will be more than double its present number; one can hazard the estimate that, by the year 2000, Latin America alone will probably have a population approaching 500 million; the United States (whose population grows somewhat more slowly) and Canada, perhaps 375 million. Taken together, this suggests a Western Hemisphere population bloc aggregating 875 million, quite capable of holding its own with the great Asian blocs which appear so impressive today and will also be much more populous a generation hence, especially since there is no direct correspondence between mere numbers and power and accomplishment: what counts is the structure of population and how it is organized.

The second fact is that there is *Lebensraum* in the hemisphere for this increasing population. Land is available for settlement, for development, for production. The natural resources of the region are great—so great indeed that we cannot yet attempt to estimate their real potential. Much of them are virgin; they have not been exploited, wasted, or depleted by thousands of years of occupation. When the hemispheric population bloc approaches a billion, as it well may shortly after the advent of the next century, the density of population will still be relatively comfortable—far less, in fact, than the density of population in Western Europe now—and the natural resources even if not augmented by science (as they probably will be) should be comfortably adequate.

The Need for Unity

In the light of these facts, there is no reason to assume that the next century will necessarily be wholly "Asian."

But this involves another assumption: that the countries occupying this American land mass, and the populations now in being and coming into being, will be able to stick together, move together, develop a consensus as to their values, and form a common civilization. This assumption is tenable, but the condition it implies is by no means inevitable. Unlike the Chinese mainland, the Latin American region is not "tied up," nor unified, nor has it attained a harmonious working relationship. Unless this is achieved, the Latin American nations could quite easily fall into the limbo in which the interstitial Asian nations from Viet-Nam to Burma and Pakistan find themselves at present. That is, they could find themselves at hazard and exposed amid the tensions and conflicts between greater powers, Asian, North American, Russian, or European, as the case might prove. No one familiar with the lot of interstitial nations—the Soviet satellite countries in Europe, or the Southeast Asian nations—would wish that misfortune on his Latin American neighbors.

Absence of a strong and harmonious working relationship

among the Latin American countries—and between them and the United States—is not altogether surprising. Until relatively recently, most of them were in fact substantial but isolated settlements in a great continent, out of contact with each other. There was little communication between them and that almost entirely by sea. The settled areas usually were and still are not contiguous. There are exceptions, of course: the common border between Argentina and Brazil brought and brings population blocs into direct contact. The countries on the Andean plateau had limited land contact in the days of the Inca Empire and have continued to have it, albeit sparsely. Yet the great communications lines cross, not in any Latin American center, but in New York or London or Paris. Until recently, their statesmen, businessmen, and cultural leaders met each other in those cities rather than in any Latin American capital, for it was easier than to undertake arduous and sometimes dangerous journeys from their own capitals even to those of their next-door neighbors.

That situation is changing now with great speed. But the change is relatively recent. The air-transport net by which Latin Americans move from one country and one city to neighboring countries and cities became effective for practical purposes only after World War II. The Pan American Highway, given powerful impetus by President Franklin Roosevelt, is only barely reaching completion. There never was, perhaps there never will be, a railroad net bringing South America together in the sense that we take for granted in the United States. Road systems able to make motor transport and travel readily available by anything on wheels are only barely begun—though they are steadily being developed at a pace undreamed of twenty years ago. Telegraph and wireless communications, of course, have moved forward to modern proportions. The isolation of the Latin American centers has indeed ended because through radio, telegraph, press coverage, and air transport, each country now lives with the knowledge and in the presence of all other countries. But this condition has only existed for about twenty years. The habit of local rather than regional action, though rapidly breaking down, still remains dominant.

Nonetheless, the slow process of building a single region goes steadily forward. The United Nations group commonly called ECLA (Economic Commission for Latin America) under the leadership of a brilliant Argentine, Raúl Prebisch, has developed plans for a Latin American common market. It is finding wide support, not merely because of the competence of the plan, but because economic developments (save in the huge country of Brazil) almost necessarily require greater markets than are offered by individual countries. On the cultural side, intellectuals of all Spanish-speaking countries avidly read each other's books. Scientific research, spreading with rapidity, by its nature depends on continuous interchange of ideas and results. While the political life of the various countries is often pathetically parochial, the underlying forces clearly move toward closer relationships whether politicians appreciate it or not. The fate of Latin America, and perhaps of the entire hemisphere, may well depend on the success or failure of the movement toward integration.

Latin America and the United States

A final observation must color this brief geopolitical survey. Relations between Latin America and the United States will determine whether the hemispheric bloc emerges as an invincible powerful force, or whether Latin America, though a substantial force, is to remain a weak, junior factor in the coming half century. If harmonious relations can be worked out between a Latin American common market and the European Common Market, clearly Latin America will be far stronger than if she tries to go it alone. To be strong at all, she must have good economic relations either with Europe or with the United States; she would attain maximum advantage from a cooperative relation with both. The choice may not be an entirely open one: Latin America is not likely to reach advantageous relations with the European Common Market unless she also has advantageous relations with the United States.

The United States, of course, has a choice, which Latin America does not. Whether or not this country is able to find a sound cooperative and mutually advantageous working relationship with Latin America—that is, a north-south axis—she can and doubtless will work out an east-west axis of comparable or greater strength. By establishing close working relationships with Canada and Western Europe, with the English-speaking members of the British Commonwealth, with the European Common Market, with the Philippines, and with Japan, she can maintain herself very well indeed.

Latin American politicians sometimes say—and others probably think—that the United States "cannot" withdraw her interest from Latin America. This is not the fact. She should not, if it can be maintained. But she "can." The United States does not need Latin America as a field of investment for her capital. There is, and increasingly will be, more than enough work for American capital at home. (About $17,000 of capital expenditure is now needed to provide one job for an American workman—and our labor force expands at the rate of two million or more a year.) Everything taken into account, American capital does not yearn to go abroad at all and does not go abroad easily. In recent years it has been difficult to induce it to enter Latin America. Nearly 80 per cent of the capital actually exported to the area has been expended for discovery and development of oil; American investors on the whole prefer to place their capital in the United States, with Canada and Europe as second and third choices.

Nor are Latin American products essential to the U.S. economy. Lenin laid down as dogma that the way to conquer the capitalist powers of Western Europe was to seize the colonial areas of Asia and Africa or cut off the supply of raw materials from those areas to the West. In the phrase so often attributed to him, "the road to Paris and London lies through Peking and Calcutta." The event proved him wrong. When the time came and these countries became independent—when the Netherlands was cut off from the East Indies, when Britain left India, Malaya and Ceylon, when France left Indo-China—Western Europe did not wither and die. To the contrary, it attained and now has a higher prosperity than ever before. So far as the United States is concerned, the domestic beet and cane sugar interests anxiously hope that all Latin American cane sugar can be excluded from the home market; they are quite able to supply the sugar now imported. Copper is not wanting in the North American continent. Most of the materials we import from Latin America either are present here or can readily be obtained elsewhere. This is even true of coffee, now available in Africa. Readjustment of American affairs to do without Latin American products would be far less difficult than the readjustment required of Britain when she voluntarily made her former colonies independent, or of the Netherlands when Indonesian independence ended her control over most of the East Indian archipelago.

The converse is not true. Latin American countries cut off from the American market would have to undergo a desperate and painful readjustment. Chile without an American market for her copper; Brazil, Colombia, and Central America without an American market for their coffee; Venezuela without American facilities for marketing her oil—all would have to reorient their economies in crisis and distress. This is a consummation devoutly not to be desired, and every Latin American economist and businessman knows it, although some political leaders do not.

Marxist-Leninist propaganda preaches, in season and out, that great nations like the United States "must" seek underdeveloped nations to exploit, else their capital has no place to go. In 1919 Lenin boasted to the Central Committee of the Communist Party that he could always influence the United States by offering her capitalists concessions to exploit Siberia; these capitalists would then influence the American government to make concessions to Russian policy to gain new fields of exploitation. Actually, modern technical development made and still makes the United States more attractive as an area of investment than any other part of the world, with the European Common Market area as the only rival in sight.

Hence many current problems. In her relations with Latin America, the United States has an alternative. She can work in the Northern Hemisphere and do extremely well at it, and plenty of politico-economic forces wish her to do so. If Latin American statesmen and politicians follow the unsubstantial slogan of an "independent" foreign policy (this was former President Jânio Quadros' idea) the United States far more easily than most Latin American countries could likewise pursue an "independent" policy. Her choice, of course, has thus far been to stay in and with the Latin American region. But if either she or the Latin American region were to choose otherwise, it would not be any unmanageable strain on the economic life of the United States.

These are the three main geopolitical considerations to be kept in mind as the United States surveys her southern neighbors. Working together the United States and Latin America should be able to create an economic and social construct capable of meeting any probable European, Asian, or African development in the next generation. It should, indeed, produce more plentifully and distribute more evenly than any other socio-economic system in the world. But this construct assumes that the region as a whole, including the United States, can be brought together in a smooth-working relationship, so that it can and will maintain itself as an integrated economic and political action group in facing the problems and conflicts which lie ahead. Absent such integration, the United States can abandon (or be forced out of) the north-south axis. Then she would, almost necessarily, give emphasis to an east-west axis running from the iron curtain to the Western Pacific. For a stable world, obviously the greatest success would be attained if she were able to develop both axes.

2. The Latin American Scene

Geopolitical possibilities are all very well; but their development is a matter of political organization. Here, unhappily, the landscape is far less promising.

Because the following observations are frankly critical, let it not be supposed either that Latin American nations are incapable of good organization or that enormous progress has not been made in the past generation. If one takes 1920 as a starting date, and compares conditions as they then stood with those of today, it is clear that country by country and throughout the whole region a civilization is being built with remarkable speed.

A striking fact is that the national product (more accurately, the regional product) grew by an average of about 4.5 per cent annually in the late 1950s,[1] whereas the gross national product

---

[1] The percentage figures are 5.9 (1955), 4.2 (1956), 6.9 (1957), 4.1 (1958), 2.8 (1959). The decline in 1959, a reflection of severe economic and social

of the United States increases only by a little more than 3 per cent. Though there are many current difficulties, the economy is productive. The verdict passed on the United States by many European observers about, let us say, 1900, was critical in the extreme. But in the United States at that time, careful analysts reasoned that the nation was on its way, though there were doubts whether progress would continue. This writer's conclusion is that Latin America is now on its way. Doubts as to its continued progress arise from the fact that, for the first time since the region became independent, progress is encountering the disruptive forces loosed by industrial revolution, by the cold war, and by attempts at Communist invasion. Absent these, the forecast would be brilliant.

But these factors are not absent. There is Communist invasion, driven by the forces producing the cold war in various degrees of intensity, in all these countries. Particular cause for concern lies perhaps in the nature of the Communist movement itself. In nearly half a century since the Russian Revolution of 1917 it has destroyed many structures. It has created only two—in the Soviet Union and in China. Outside the borders of those predominantly Slavic and Oriental empires there is not a single instance in which processes of Communist revolution have yet created viable civilization. Further, communism in power is an organization for the maintenance and the expansion of power: its validity in Latin America is tested chiefly by the extent to which revolutions acknowledge and obey the orders of the imperialism of Moscow or Peiping. What we are seeing now is a group of twenty independent Latin American states in all of which attempts are being made to disrupt the present social order by supposedly revolutionary forces which have yet to demonstrate capacity to construct anything effective in the place of the formations they destroy, and whose chief emphasis is on combating the United States and entering the Soviet or Red Chinese empires. The destructive process is aimed not merely at the stability

strains, was followed by a rise of 3.7 per cent in 1960. See U.N. Economic and Social Council, *Economic Survey of Latin America 1959*, E/CN.12/541, June 14, 1960, p. 57; same, *1960*, Part One, E/CN.12/565, March 1, 1961, p. 5.

of the states themselves but at the continuance of the arrangements between those states which have thus far formed the nucleus of organization in the Pan American world.

An added difficulty in any analysis is the fact that Latin America is undergoing not one revolution, but two. Quite aside from Communist movements, there is a real and continuing indigenous effort, found everywhere in the region, which asserts greater rights of participation in government, in production, and in wealth for the Latin American masses. This is as endemic as it is justified. Its roots go back to the French Revolution. Its thinking originally was primarily political, and only later was economic as well. From the days of Simón Bolívar through the Mexican Revolution which began in 1910 to the revolutions in progress now in Venezuela, Bolivia, and elsewhere, the essential drive has not changed.

The advent of the Communist movement, which entered the hemisphere in the thirties and to some extent established itself during the Second World War, complicated the indigenous revolution. The Communists tried to link *any* revolutionary movement aimed at human betterment with a hatred—hatred of the United States as somehow responsible for the ills of the Latin American countries. For the past decade Communist propaganda and teaching in Latin America have been far more concerned with spreading hatred of the United States than with indicating lines of reconstruction or of new development. Methods of class war were adapted to become methods of warfare against the United States. What will be done in any country in the event that warfare succeeds, few people discuss.

The result is a variety of three-cornered conflict. On the one side are conservatives, families who have owned land and plantations, augmented by a newer and often more powerful group which has emerged in many countries by organizing industry and finance. The second force may be called liberal—that is, it is not Marxist though conceivably it may become so. It is sometimes called the "non-Communist left." Its real interest lies in changing the social and economic life of the country in very much the manner by which the social and economic life of the United States was changed by the New Deal of President Franklin Roosevelt. The third or Communist group has no use for either, intends to destroy both, but follows the tactical lines often including "common fronts" with elements of one of the other groups, calculated to forward its advantage. Tactics do not exclude, and often favor, temporary alliances with its most reactionary targets.

In Europe in the decade of the thirties, Communist movements sometimes made common cause with the extreme right for the purpose of eliminating the non-Communist left and liberal groups. The Hitler-Stalin alliance was the most spectacular instance. More often, attempts were made to present the only possible political choice as between fascism and communism, no third way being possible; this was designed to annex liberals or Socialists to Communist leadership in a "popular front." Very much this process is being repeated in Latin America in the decade of the sixties. For example, the Cuban revolution of 1957-58 was in no sense Communist. It was carried out by the middle class and by left-of-center, but non-Communist, labor groups. It was successful precisely because the Cuban dictatorship under Batista was singularly vulnerable. The speed with which the Communist groups, having succeeded to power in 1959, destroyed any liberal movements was characteristic.

Elsewhere, and especially where reactionary governments were strong, as in the case of the Dominican Republic under the Trujillo dictatorship, the first Communist objective was to wipe out the democratic middle. There, however, the successful betrayal of Cuba's revolution of the 26th of July by Fidel Castro and his Communist allies may have suggested a change of tactics. Evidence is not wanting of an attempt at turning the trick of betraying a non-Communist, anti-Trujillo revolution into the hands of a small, organized, and powerfully armed Communist minority. One would not like to insure the lives of the non-Communists lured into these united fronts in case of Communist success.

In the context of this three-cornered conflict we may look briefly at the three largest of our neighbors.

Mexico

The nearest is Mexico, whose thirty-six million people have been integrated by a successful revolution which began forty years ago. In Latin America it ranks after Brazil as the second most populous and powerful country in the region. Mexico's government is democratic in a general sense, though with a single-party system that is peculiarly Mexican. There are, of course, other parties including a Communist party; but the Partido Revolucionario Institucional has a hold on most of Mexico comparable in some ways to the hold which the Democratic party has classically held in many of the southern states of the United States. Political issues are discussed and decisions taken within the party and ratified rather than decided through the process of national election. The Partido Revolucionario Institucional is beginning to be a battleground itself. The left wing, headed by the veteran general and former president, Lázaro Cárdenas, has been considering covertly, and sometimes overtly, alliance with the Communist movement and espousal of a new revolution somewhat similar to that of Fidel Castro in Cuba. The majority of the Partido Revolucionario does not accept that idea. President Adolfo López Mateos, probably wisely, has endeavored to keep the conflict between the two wings of the party from reaching the stage of open contest.

The resulting situation is typical of many Latin American governments: an administration whose component individuals do not wish evolution along Communist lines, but who hesitate to force any issue which may divide their party and precipitate open conflict in their country. When any problem arises which would force square confrontation, every effort is made to avoid the issue. It is too easy to dismiss this policy as mere political cowardice. Unquestionably politicians fear the bitter, unscrupulous, and personal attacks to which they are exposed whenever they emerge as direct opponents of policies advocated by Communists in their own country, or by the Soviet Union or China outside. And, quite honestly, statesmen in that situation fear to decide issues which may divide their countries, possibly to the stage of civil war, which Communist parties contemplate as entirely permissible or desirable. No one knows better than these statesmen that where, when, and to the extent possible force can be used, the Communist tactic is to use it.

Hispanic America, like Spain, has a latent capacity for civil war. In circumstances offering possibility that that latent capacity will be unleashed, political leaders may be forgiven for hesitancy. Americans might usefully recall the hesitation of their own politicians in the six years before the firing on Fort Sumter signaled the outbreak of the War between the States. Of course, there is little historical reason to believe that avoidance of issues averts the conflict: more often, the longer the avoidance the worse the eventual conflict.

The Mexican problem is typical in another respect. Mexico's actual economic progress is remarkable. She is rapidly approaching or has already reached the stage christened as "take-off" by Walt Rostow in his brilliant *Stages of Economic Growth*. Industrialization, almost unknown forty years ago, is proceeding rapidly in the great Mexican cities, notably in the Mexico City region. Increasingly Mexico is attaining capacity to manufacture for her own markets. Interestingly enough, in large part this has been made possible by her cooperation with the United States. Far from being disadvantageous, the more recent American investment in her country has commonly been made in partnership with Mexicans. It presents relatively little threat that her resources and productivity will be dominated by foreigners. In general, Mexican employment and Mexican labor as well as the Mexican consumer have profited by the cooperation. This is in marked contrast to the somewhat moribund condition of the Mexican oil fields, taken over from the British and American oil companies twenty years ago and nationalized through a state oil monopoly. Whatever may be said, most Mexicans know that the presence of a powerful and well-disposed American economy to the north has helped and not hurt Mexican growth, and that obstacles to that growth are inherently Mexican and not foreign.

There is also a special type of nationalism, even as regards revolutions. The Mexican Revolution of 1910 preceded the Russian. It was home-grown and home-developed. It made its own theories. It developed its own policies. Few Mexicans like to be told that they need another revolution invented abroad. There is also a vivid memory of the horrors of the ensuing civil war period, which for practical purposes did not end until 1928. Eighteen years of sporadic guerrilla warfare leave a bitter mark; that kind of experience a country does not readily wish to repeat.

In result, the Communists have been successful primarily with the intellectuals. Communist thinking is perhaps more firmly entrenched in the University of Mexico than in any other Latin American center; certainly it is more firmly entrenched there than in any other part of Mexico. That is where it will continue to have its main force, unless, of course, some powerful leader throws his personal following into its ideological and political grip.

Brazil

Brazil, the largest country in Latin America, is unique. It is Portuguese by language, tradition, and habit of action. It does not readily turn to violence; historically, its government has been more stable than those even of Western Europe. The instinct of compromise is greater even than that of Anglo-Saxons, and friendships are not blocked by party lines. Yet, in part, these things are so because Brazilians have demanded less of their government; a vast expanse (about equal to the United States minus Alaska but plus a second Texas) made individual and local development easy and centralized control difficult. In the Brazilian proverb, the country progresses at night because the government is then asleep. This expresses a widely held attitude. Some of Brazil's current political difficulties arise from the fact that modern communication and economic processes are forcing the country into centralization, while governmental and administrative methods and habits are not quite ready to cope with the resulting problems. Particularly in the great interior, trade, development, and economic life go on without government intervention, as far and fast as they can—which is considerable.

Whatever Brazil's attitudes in the field of foreign affairs, the real preoccupation of the country is the conquest of its own west, as was the case in the United States from the Civil War to the actual development of the Pacific Coast. When that development was achieved at the end of the nineteenth century, the United States became significant on the world scene as a result of the Spanish-American War. When Brazilian development has reached its western limit at the Andes, say a generation hence, we should expect an equivalent emergence. Meanwhile, on the frontier of their settled area, running from the Amazon forest edge to the boundary at Paraguay, Brazilians are steadily reducing wilderness to farm land and villages which ten years later are small but substantial cities. The newly opened capital at Brasilia was intended to give impetus to this western march—and unquestionably will do so.

Presently, the political organization of the country is in full transition. The election of President Quadros was a real expression of popular will. His resignation, whatever his motive, was regarded as desertion by great numbers who had accepted him as leader. The Vice-President who succeeded, now President João Goulart, had no comparable popular following and his previous statements had been resented in army circles. The army has been unjustly accused of fascism in opposing him; its real reason was desire to protect the democracy won when the army (with the backing of the country) compelled Getulio Vargas to end his dictatorship in 1945.

To maintain the constitution and yet not give power to a president thought to have dictatorial ambitions was the problem. In typical Brazilian fashion a compromise was reached: the vice-president would become president (as he has done), but the country would be governed by a cabinet responsible to Congress. Since this was obviously a transition arrangement, there was to be a plebiscite before the next election determining whether the president was to enjoy centralized powers (like the president of the United States) or was to be a ceremonial official (like the president of France before the Gaullist period). Of necessity this compromise foreshadowed a government not secure in its authority until the next turn of affairs, while all the parties might be expected to try to consolidate their respective positions. These are the classic Democrats (National Democratic Union), the second largest party; the Social Democrats (in actual fact the conservative party despite their name), the largest; and the Labor party, to which Goulart belongs, third in size but still a substantial contender. Since the Communist party is illegal, its representation is split among the other parties, the Communists' most consistent opponents being in the National Democratic Union.

Meanwhile, each of the Brazilian states maintains its own organization and attracts some of the ablest younger men of the country. The government of the state of São Paulo, from the governor down to his youngest cabinet minister, has attracted ability of a caliber commanding respect anywhere in the world. The same is true of the state of Guanabara (Rio de Janeiro and environs). Able men govern the states of Bahia and Minas Gerais. Whatever its difficulties, Brazil has a reservoir of able, well-educated, and trained young men beginning to fill the vacuum inevitably resulting from the Vargas dictatorship.

The cold war has come to Brazil, though not yet quite openly. Working by the "united front" technique, Communist propaganda elected to use "nationalism" as a mask, a classic Leninist formula. Exploiting some real problems and inventing a great many more, this propaganda has attempted to portray the United States as responsible for the ills brought on Brazil by a frankly inflationary policy. Some in the nationalist movement know that they are acting as Communist cat's-paws; most probably do not.

The weak point, politically as well as economically, is the great tropical northeast shoulder of Brazil, inhabited by perhaps twelve million people. Much of this is forbidding land, semi or intermittently desert where standards of living are fatefully low. This is the legacy of the civilization described by Gilberto Freyre in his classic, *The Masters and the Slaves*. Here there is an active movement for agrarian reform—a reform obviously needed; but some of the leaders of that movement are probably Communists practicing the Chinese "Yenan way." There are indications of organization for an eventual guerrilla campaign purely in the interests of the Communists, whose ultimate end does not correspond to those of the peasants intended to furnish the gun fodder and is concealed from them. A gifted young Brazilian industrialist, Israel Klabin, studied this situation and financed the work of Celso Furtado in drawing the "northeast plan" which is now being put into effect with government support.

Brazil will go forward. Its national product has nearly doubled since 1950 and increased by 6 per cent in 1960.[2] In contrast to 1945, when most manufactured articles were imported, it now manufactures efficiently most of the products it needs, from motor cars to newsprint, from steel to ceramics. The Brazilian economy is at or near the "take-off point," much as was the United States in 1900. Granted even a reasonable measure of government stability, fiscal responsibility, and honest, socially conscious administration, it should have an explosion of progress in the next decade, bringing it alongside the West European nations.

Argentina

Finally, Argentina. This, originally the most progressive and ambitious of Latin American countries, is at the moment liquidating the political and social heritage of the fascist regime of Juan Domingo Perón. His rule was economically disastrous: in addition to adopting wasteful economic policies, he and his associates systematically plundered a rich country of many hundreds of millions of dollars, much of which was prudently cached in Switzerland. A substantial and formidable Peronista organization remains politically active in the country. The formula of government-controlled labor unions capable of being converted into demonstrating or perhaps revolting mobs, plus a doctrine of *justicialismo* (Italian fascism by another name), retains a certain strength because, as under fascism, great numbers of workers did get special benefits and were convinced their interests were served and protected by the system, and because ambitious men found in the movement an avenue to fame and power. It was not always evident that the real interests of labor were being defeated by Perón's manipulations, his systematic plundering the country of its capital, and the carnival of corruption in his administration.

Democracy returned to Argentina, as to Brazil, via the army

[2] U.N. Economic Commission for Latin America, *Economic Bulletin for Latin America: Statistical Supplement*, v. 5 (Santiago de Chile: Author, 1960), p. 24; *Economic Survey of Latin America 1960*, Part One, cited, p. 10.

and the navy. The armed forces ended the Perón dictatorship in 1955, then supported an interim government headed by General Aramburu, who promised and faithfully held an honest free election. It was won by President Arturo Frondizi, leader of the "Intransigent" wing that had broken off from the historic Radical party and a convinced democrat, although the votes of the Peronistas were an important element in his winning total. The "Popular" Radical party, in opposition, probably commands equal or nearly equal strength.

The Peronistas have traffic with the Communists. They may even be in direct alliance with them. Students of Latin American affairs are familiar with this standard Communist gambit. After taking office, Frondizi himself, attempting a necessary but unpopular austerity program for economic stabilization and growth, no longer had Peronista support and sought to bolster an essentially weak position by balancing various groups within his own party and with the opposition, endeavoring not to precipitate open and sharply divisive issues. But always in the background were the Argentine army and navy whose leaders will not tolerate a Peronista return or a Communist orientation, but do not want a military dictatorship either if they can possibly avoid it.

In addition, President Frondizi tried to appeal to a classic Argentine ambition—to lead South America as the United States leads North America. This is why, in the long run, Argentina rarely follows Brazil's lead, though transitory arrangements are familiar. Argentine nationalism is a theme played upon by the Communists, but its roots are of indigenous origin, just as there was a period of fascist-type dictatorship in Argentina in the nineteenth century long before Hitler's agents got around to backing the movement which took power with Perón in 1943.

One cannot look at Argentina without being impressed by her reserve of power. Buenos Aires is as big a city as Paris. Argentina's industrial construction is impressive. Her agricultural resources are unmatched. Her oil resources supply the larger part of the country's needs, and should soon supply all. Hispanic with strong Italian and German admixture, Argentina has a threshold of violence more easily crossed than in Brazil, and its dictatorships can be brutal. The difficulties of Argentine statesmen in endeavoring to liquidate *Peronismo* and make the democratic system work command sympathy and must enjoin understanding. In the future, Argentina is likely to become a vastly larger north-of-Italy, fecund, productive, prosperous and powerful, though geopolitically overshadowed by her huge northern neighbor.

* * *

No vignette sketches can do justice to countries as countries. The three here outlined have brought into existence intellectual, artistic, musical, and political achievements of first rank. They will continue to do so. Particularly in Argentina and Brazil, this very fact is not far removed from possible tragedy. The tradition of the French Revolution is strong in South America. One remembers the splendid young men of Italy who in 1800 intrigued with the revolutionary government of France to produce political change in their own country. In that hope they formed cadres which presently became "fifth columns" for the French armies. They were promptly betrayed into the predatory and fatal grip of the Napoleonic Empire. Anyone familiar with the opera *Tosca* has seen in melodramatic form the fate of these young men—the fantastic, terrible tragedy of idealistic and sincere revolution betrayed by an imperial power.

In Latin America, of course, the Napoleonic armies did not penetrate. The Monroe Doctrine helped to prevent later counterrevolution that might have destroyed newly won independence. Today, there are young men in Mexico, in Brazil, and in Argentina who are reverting to the pattern of the young men at the time of the French Revolution—save that they think of Moscow or Peiping as young men in 1800 thought of Paris. To Americans, well informed as to the ultimate designs of both Peiping and Moscow, the road to betrayal of these ideals has already been cynically charted; even the names of the men are duly recorded in the appropriate Communist intelligence offices, probably with a note that they are to be used up to a certain point, after which they are to be liquidated. To give them a fair chance to be, not puppets of propaganda or tools in the hands of an outside power, but actual proponents of a social movement for the betterment of their own countries must be one of the preoccupations of every friend Latin America has in the United States.

Chapter II

Social Change, Revolutionary Governments, and Extra-Continental Power Politics

Social change, in the context of Latin America, involves the possibility, perhaps the probability, that new governments will be established by revolution. These may do more than merely change the administration of the government. They may change its social system. We must anticipate that, in some countries, social systems will arise or will be imposed wholly different from those to which we are accustomed.

Intellectuals in many of these countries frequently make a telling observation. Surveying the contrast between great wealth and abject poverty, they make a charge. If, they say, this is what Christian civilization produces ("Christian civilization" means substantially what in the United States is meant by "Western civilization"), it has failed. The real task is to construct a new civilization on a new theory and a new base. Not infrequently such comments are prelude to an argument in favor of Communist revolution, although not because of any conversion to Marxism or any liking for the tyranny that exists in Communist states. They reflect a passionate desire to escape, somehow, from the nineteenth-century organization of affairs out of which current Latin American life seems to provide no exit save by revolution.

North Americans do not readily understand this. We ourselves have never adequately formulated the theory and method of the social-economic system prevailing in the United States. In its own empiric fashion, the United States has developed a system which relegates Marxian communism to the museum of nineteenth-century thought. That is, we have at one and the same time achieved a vast increase of production, a vast increase of distribution, and an enduring system of individual liberty. We have done this peacefully. This made it possible for the United States to abolish the proletariat, rather than to enthrone it. The United States had a long head start resulting from a century and a half of compulsory, free, common education—a condition which does not exist in much of Latin America today—and the fruits of a great deal of experimentation in the various state and local governments. But we have never explained those processes in readily understandable theory.

In much of Latin America, at all events, revolution must be reckoned as a possibility, and major and rapid evolution is a necessity. We can hope and pray that the process of change will not entail decades of civil strife and disorder like the Mexican Revolution or the kind of civil war which decimated Spain in the decade of the nineteen thirties. But we can have no certainty that Latin America will escape terrible ordeals of this kind. At that point the problems of the United States in her Latin American relations will become even more acute.

Very possibly we shall see social systems emerging in some parts of Latin America (especially in the Andean plateau populated by Indians) completely strange to our own institutions and ways of thinking. How best can the United States determine its position?

The United States and the New Regimes

To this writer, an implacable criterion of judgment has to be that of the safety of the United States. The fact that a new order is different or unfamiliar to us is wholly secondary in importance to the question whether it is, in the context of the prevailing world struggle, dangerous to our own survival. The United States can, and during most of its existence has, coexisted quite happily with all manner of social systems governed by all manner of political organization. It is, for example, quite possible to imagine systems not based on the institution of private property (though we might be dubious about their success), and for the United States to work happily with them—provided they do not assert as a necessary concomitance that they must join with others in conquering the United States, or insist (as Castro does) that they will, in some fashion, attack the American political-economic system. For a period of nearly twenty years, the Soviet Union has coexisted with Finland, whose system bears no relation at all to the Communist system—being assured that a non-Communist Finland represented no danger to the safety of the Soviet Union. But she would not tolerate Finland's entry into, or association with, NATO.

The United States would undoubtedly have its own views as to the desirability or prospects of these new systems. It maintained peaceful relations with the feudal despotism of Trujillo in the Dominican Republic, in the stability and results of which the United States had no confidence whatever. Active hostility on the official level really began when Trujillo undertook murderous intrigues outside his own country. The United States could, and in the opinion of this writer should, maintain wholly friendly relations with a Socialist regime, if that regime were willing to be friendly with the United States and to keep hemispheric peace. The United States has been able to do such with the current revolutionary government of Bolivia, whose regime indeed has been powerfully assisted because of that friendship. There would have been no great difficulty in maintaining similar friendly relations with Castro's Cuba had not Castro, according to his own statement a Leninist conspirator working with the Soviet Union, intentionally picked a quarrel with the United States at the behest and in the interest of an extra-continental Communist power.

A second criterion must be the attitude of a revolution and a revolutionary government toward human rights. The relationship here is in the nature of things rather than a matter to be decided as diplomatic policy. A revolution like Hitler's, which asserted the virtue of massacring all Jews, automatically set up a current of public opinion in the United States preventing any pretense of good relations. A regime falling below a certain standard of civilization automatically brings into play emotional forces. In a democracy like the United States these forces powerfully influence policy. The torture chambers in Ciudad Trujillo embittered relations between the Dominican Republic and its neighbors, including the United States, long before the Dominican plot against Venezuela.

The problem of human rights is not as easily solved as would appear. Excuses for cruelty, savagery, and even sheer sadism have had ghastly repetition throughout the whole of this generation. They are sometimes excused as transient incidents of the process of revolution. They are sometimes justified as a necessary slaughter or elimination of incompatibles—for example, Stalin's condemnation of several million Ukrainians to death by starvation and his "plowing under" of entire nationality groups in the U.S.S.R. These justifications have never commanded confidence either in Latin America or the United States. An excellent guide book to what is expected in the way of respect for human rights is contained in the "American Declaration of the Rights and Duties of Man," agreed at Bogotá in 1948. Though this document states an ideal rather than a common denominator of opinion, reference to it sufficiently indicates a consensus in the Americas as to what should be, and even more clearly indicates minimum standards, violation of which puts a regime beyond the pale of civilized countries.

The third criterion relates to the international conduct of a revolutionary regime. It should be expected to keep the peace and refrain from attempting to extend its system beyond its borders. A regime that considers itself free, in the name of its revolutionary morality, to attack its neighbors at once gives rise to the countervailing right of any other country in the neighborhood to return the attack. Since one of them is the United States, the considerations are serious. Revolutionary aggression or imperialism is no more entitled to respect than any other kind.

This prospect poses problems. Revolutions do not always mind their own business in their own countries. The Castro regime had barely established itself before attacking in quick succession the Dominican Republic, the republic of Panama, and the republic of Guatemala.

When a regime conforms to the three criteria—(1) that it does not make itself a danger to the United States, (2) that it does not violate at least minimal standards of human rights, and (3) that it does not undertake aggression against its neighbors—there should be wide understanding and tolerance. The tolerance, let it be added, cannot be unlimited. A dictatorial government does not allow self-determination to its people. In the nature of things there will be doubt whether such a regime speaks for its people, or for its guns. For the United States also, there must always be realization that dictatorial regimes do come to an end, and, when they do, the friends of the regime are stigmatized as enemies by the people who were ruled by it.

The point, quite simply, is that a regime which is not capitalist nor based on private property, but otherwise observes the laws of nations, of humanity, and of the hemisphere, need not be an unwelcome member of the American family of nations. The inter-American system was not founded to defend capitalism or any other social system. It was founded to keep old-world powers from extending their intrigues and their domination into the new world; to defend the right of the peoples of the American nations to build their own political and social systems; and to maintain peace within the hemisphere.

The Communist Threat and the Need for Action

The thorniest and most acute problems which will face the United States arise out of the nature of the change which may occur in some parts of Latin America. The situation could offer possibility of a number of civil wars. On December 9, 1961, Castro called for two—in Colombia and Venezuela. In January 1962, during the Punta del Este Conference, he attempted three—in Venezuela, in Guatemala, in Nicaragua. Others are possible. Civil wars, if they can be fomented and occur at the same time, conceivably might aggregate in certain areas. They may not eventuate, but the potential is present. Such a design has been proclaimed by Cuba, and it ought not to be ignored. Saving as much of the American hemisphere as possible from the sheer horror involved in that kind of warfare should be a part of U.S. policy, so far as that policy can be effective, although capacity of the

United States to assist peaceful solution of internal struggles within Latin American countries must of necessity be extremely limited.

The potentially bloody character of struggles for social change can, of course, be modified by statesmanship where Communists are not principal contenders. Where they are, their dogma imposes force in seizing power and its attainment is only the beginning and not the end of killing. In all successful Communist revolutions to date, in any part of the world, the blood shed by the ensuing government *after* it was successful in establishing its power has been greater than the death toll incurred in the course of its effort. Cuba is a current illustration. The prescribed "class war" must be carried through to its bloody end.

In some areas "classes" are differently defined. The Communist instructions regarding Haiti, for example, have little to do with economics; they direct that every mulatto (as also every white man) in the country must be considered a "class enemy." Elsewhere, classes scheduled for abolition will be otherwise identified —probably on the basis of previous condition of birth, land ownership, or position in the community. The prospect is not pretty.

Still less pretty is the fact that in these possible externally fomented civil wars one side will so far as possible be directly financed, armed, and assisted from outside the continent by extra-continental powers whose primary effort will be to establish their ultimate control, and in the process to direct as much hatred as possible against the United States. This means that one of the two—or perhaps three (if Communist China be included)—contending forces will be an enemy of the United States and also will be receiving help from the Soviet Union or Communist China, perhaps from both. It would be sheer unreality to pretend that the United States was not concerned in the outcome. One of the slogans in any case will be that the insurgents intend to "liberate" their country from the United States. By this is meant that immediately American investments, if any, in the country will be confiscated, and (of more seriousness) that the country itself will be promptly placed under the control of one or the other of the two Communist powers as ally in a struggle against the United States. Precisely because conquest by the overseas

Communist powers is intended, the purely spurious charge will be made that the armed insurgence is needed to "defend" the country from the United States.

The instinct of most Americans, in government and out, is to back away from these situations. The reason is clear enough. Having no shadow of interest in colonialism, the first reaction is that the United States has nothing to defend—it simply is not a party. Second thoughts are apt to bring a different conclusion. A country "liberated" by the Communists is, in fact, a new-world state suffering an armed attack from outside. That attack, by the Rio Treaty, is an attack on all American states, whether they recognize it or not. Once that diagnosis is made, the United States is forced to consider the interest of her own defense as well as the defense of the country involved. Communist propaganda will not make this easy. It will be asserted at once that any assistance given by the United States to any non-Communist faction is merely for the purpose of defending capitalist interests there, or latifundia landlords, or reactionaries, or past dictators, or what you will. The fact that none of this has any relation to truth will not prevent a rising tide of calumny as unlimited in bitterness and volume as in mendacity.

The United States, of course, has faced these situations before. Just such a tide of abuse was loosed in 1947 when President Truman picked up the burden of the defense of Greece against Communist attack. President Truman dealt with it with a salty brusqueness useful to remember. Where propaganda is concerned, in Latin America as elsewhere Communists are usually better at dishing it out than at taking it. Solid counterattack is the best policy. Merely dropping out of the situation will promptly be interpreted as meaning that the United States has abandoned defense of the inter-American system and deserted her friends in their moment of need.

The danger of these situations perhaps can be reduced if, in advance, the United States will state a position. This, in the somewhat analogous situation in Europe and the Near East, President Truman did by enunciating the "Truman Doctrine." Struggles of the kind outlined commonly do not break out unless the organizers of the attack believe they can win. The Nazi plot to take over Uruguay in 1939-40, ended when President Roosevelt sent the "Indianapolis" on a "courtesy visit" to Montevideo, allowing it to be known at the same time that if the President of Uruguay needed its assistance, it was immediately available. Either the United States intends to defend the hemispheric system or she does not; if she does, a great deal can be gained by making this plain from the outset. But, simultaneously it must be made plain that the purpose of the United States is to defend the self-determination of the hemisphere. Social reform, like democracy (to paraphrase Winston Churchill's remark at the time of the Greek civil war), is not to be picked up, monopolized, and made the sole property of handfuls of extremists with overseas tommy-guns. In point of fact the outcome of instigated civil wars throughout the continent is anything but a foregone conclusion. Some may assume the character of the Spanish civil war, with the Soviet Union and Communist China playing the part played in that bloody tragedy by Nazi Germany and Mussolini's Italy.

In the writer's view, it would be preferable to anticipate issues rather than merely await their development. The most hazardous policy would be to await crisis—and then see what could be done. The safety of Greece, and with it of large parts of Europe, was really assured when the British recognized the Greek civil war for what it was and promptly met the threat, though it was the United States that finished the job. Had Allied diplomacy then merely followed the turn of events, it seems almost certain that the Soviet Union would have been firmly planted in the Eastern Mediterranean long before the Marshall Plan had become effective.

Americans dislike and are not accustomed to thinking of hemispheric policy in these terms. Issues like those now appearing in Latin America have thus far been presented in areas as far away as Laos or Lebanon. They were not so directly connected with the safety of the United States, nor were the people of those countries people with whom we had agreed so specifically by treaty to make common cause—as we have done with the Latin American peoples through the Organization of American States. In the Western Hemisphere, substantial threat does exist to our national security and survival. And there we have made agreements and commitments which require that we take a position.

A final observation is crucial. The policy of the United States should not—indeed cannot—be directed toward preventing revolution. Its real task is to promote social change, if possible without violence, and to prevent revolution from being betrayed into the prehensile grip of the overseas imperialist Communist powers. Far from opposing social change, American policy can and must aim toward defending and protecting it.

This policy should not bring the United States' interests into conflict with the national interests of any country which might be involved. It will cause conflict—unavoidably—between the United States and those elements which knowingly intend to deliver their countries into the hands of a Moscow or a Peiping power complex.

The Monroe Doctrine in its time protected the early nineteenth-century revolutions from being succeeded by new revolutions fomented in the interest of Spain and the Holy Alliance powers. The Soviet Union, and more recently, Communist China are establishing a colonial empire on a vast scale, and according to the resolutions of their Communist congresses they intend to include Latin America in it. Like the Napoleonic Empire, and indeed like the Holy Alliance empires, the Communist powers are not prepared to engage in full-scale war with the United States to achieve this result. Diplomatically, and by threat and other means, including money, arms, trained experts, and intrigue, they will foment and support those elements in Latin American revolutions which they believe will bind those countries into their political system. These will be the elements most anxious to quarrel with the United States, and least anxious to permit the countries in question to establish a purely indigenous, uncontrolled system of self-government.

Chapter III

Economics and Politics

Analysis of the combination of economics and social problems in Latin America is obviously impossible in as brief a sketch as this. A quantity of adequate data and analysis is readily available on Latin American economic problems.[1] Unhappily, discussions of Latin American economics commonly proceed from a political rather than a technical economic base. Perhaps rightly so, nevertheless, because aggregate figures of economic output and growth give little guide to the human aspects and results of the system.

On the whole the Latin American economic scene is not as black as commonly presented. There has been a slow but steady increase in gross product, and, more important, a rather rapid increase in capacity to produce different kinds of products—notably essential manufactures such as steel. The industrial production of Argentina, despite the political instability there, stood in mid-1961 at or close to its all-time high (a peak reached in mid-1958) and appears to be increasing. Both industrial production and real per capita income in Mexico have been rising steadily, although the rise in income, from slightly more than $110 per capita in 1950 to $140 in 1960, indicates progress rather than affluence. Probably the greatest increase of production is in Brazil, though the statistics do not adequately reflect the immense increase in output whose product is cleared and settled land. Brazil's

[1] The Chase Manhattan Bank, for example, has produced a series of first-rate studies, *Latin American Business Highlights*, published quarterly, which rightly do not neglect political considerations. Reports prepared under the auspices of the United Nations, especially its Economic Commission for Latin America, are particularly valuable.

annual conquests of parts of her western wilderness represent productivity on a large scale.

In countries of lesser size, most show solid achievement. Mention must be made of the development of steel and electric power in the Caroni region of Venezuela; of the initiation of manufacturing on a substantial scale in Peru; of many solid achievements in Chile. Generalizations are impossible in a region the size of Latin America. But it can be said that in great areas the moment for a take-off into twentieth-century industrial production is readily visible on the horizon. In some countries, notably Brazil, Mexico, and Argentina, that point has arrived. Granted internal order, the results are likely to be spectacular within the next few years. We are thus seeing the emergence of new industrial centers capable of rivaling in speed of growth the much heralded development in the Soviet Union, far ahead of current developments in Communist China, and destined to rank with the economic achievements of Europe and the United States in another generation.

This is all very well as far as it goes. But statistics do not satisfy current human needs or calm human emotions. That is done by the social system distributing the products; more importantly, perhaps, by the estimate of that social system made by the individuals composing it. Populations put up cheerfully with great hardship when they believe the socio-political system under which they live is doing its best to improve their situation. Failing such confidence, even (or perhaps especially) in an improving economic situation, dissatisfaction may rise to the point of revolution.

In the writer's view, many of the usual clichés do not hold. Revolution is *not* a result of poverty per se. The first Communist revolution in the Western Hemisphere—Cuba—occurred in one of the richest of the Latin American republics, the distribution of whose income indicates that the average man was far better off there than elsewhere throughout the region, Puerto Rico always excepted. If stability were the only value, great poverty, great ignorance, and complete tyranny carried on by a reasonably sensitive and intelligent dictatorship might serve quite well. That is, until the eventual explosion. Tyrannies, however, are not as a

rule either sensitive or efficient. Sodden ignorance is readily interrupted by modern radio communication. Poverty, acceptable if
no other form of life has ever been known, ceases to be tolerable
when it is assumed to be the result of a system capable of doing
better, and when the poor are aware of the fact that a better
condition is possible. All these awarenesses are present in most if
not all parts of Latin America now.

We here discuss therefore the main political issues which have
arisen out of the social and economic conditions in Latin America.
Conflicts resulting from these issues are the active fronts in U.S.-
Latin American relations.

Capital: Formation, Inflow, Outflow

Almost universally throughout Latin America, there is talk of
the urgent requirements for "capital" from outside. It is said,
with accuracy, that there is immense need for funds with which
to build two kinds of permanent plant.

Public works (roads, schools, water supply, sanitation, transpor-
tation, electricity), sometimes called "social capital," form the
bulk of one of these classifications. Capital expenditures for
plants of heavy and light industry whose product is designed for
sale, such as steel mills, fabricators of various forms of commodities, and factories for consumer goods, make up the second classi-
fication. Obviously, these plants may be private, as they usually
are in the United States, or may be publicly owned—as, for example, are the steel plants in Argentina and in Venezuela. There
is little doubt about the need for capital in both classifications.

But it is not so true that local capital is nonexistent in Latin
American countries. To the contrary, there is a great deal of
Latin American capital, remaining even after the really spectacular thefts of capital on a large scale during the dictatorial era
which virtually ended in 1961. A major difficulty here is that
Latin American capital, or at least many Latin American capitalists, have been of relatively little help in the industrial development of these countries. Paradoxically, private Latin American
interests, and the governments of these countries, besiege Washington and Wall Street seeking funds which they themselves are

unwilling to use when indigenously formed or owned. Capital can be and is being formed in Latin America by Latin Americans. But, aside from real estate development, it does not automatically flow into the development of the country where formed.

Like all such generalizations, this one is unjust to many Latin American businessmen and capitalists. The writer thinks immediately of one very great industrial empire in Brazil whose controlling owners have never withdrawn or squandered profits, have steadily dedicated them to new industrial developments, and have as matter of policy refused to locate them in safe havens in New York or Switzerland. In all Latin American countries businessmen are found who consider it a matter of patriotism as well as of common sense to use the profits they have built into capital as a fund for further development of the resources of the country which gave them birth or residence. Unhappily, this sentiment is not dominant. The mentality of many of the capitalist groups in the region is the mentality of capitalists in Europe a hundred years ago.

The reasons why locally formed capital is not available to the extent it should be for economic growth are several.

The first and simplest is probably inherited habit, passing but still strong. Latin Americans do not normally think of wealth as liquid. A wealthy man has a fortune—in land, in cattle, in plantations, more recently in urban real estate, far less often in securities of industrial enterprise. Thanks in part to a system of taxation which makes their customary form of holding property relatively riskless and inexpensive, the older group of rich men find unacceptable the risks involved in holding equities in factories and industrial plants. Conservative property owners have shied away from this form of investment, very much as, in older times, conservative investors in the United States shied away from anything more risky than first mortgages.

A second obstacle to use of Latin American capital by Latin Americans in Latin America has been a strange idea of the rate of return to be derived from it. In all Latin America until recently, and in most countries now, an investor considers himself positively ill used if he does not receive a minimum interest rate of 12 per cent on a gilt-edged security—for example, a first mortgage on real property—and throughout much of the region the expected minimum rate of return is nearer 20 than 12. When the investment is not gilt-edged—for example, as in the equity stock of an industrial enterprise—the investor assumes as a matter of course that dividends of at least 20 per cent on his investment will begin at once, and he expects these to rise rather rapidly. An expectation of 40 to 50 per cent return is frequent. If pressed, the investor would argue that his return must compensate not merely for the use of his capital but also for the fact that such investments are not liquid in the same sense that investment in the stock of an American corporation is liquid through the machinery of the stock exchange. Also, he runs the chance that the money he receives will depreciate. Therefore, he must receive a rate of return allowing him to recoup his capital within a very short time, say three or four years.

Obviously, enterprises which can distribute this sort of dividend must be operating in a field at which the price they charge for their product is high in relation to the actual cost of production. This makes for a narrow market. Further, they are then not in a position to accumulate earnings (since they are expected to distribute them) and thus build industrial capital, as is the case in the United States. Industrial enterprises in the United States have been, among other things, machines for accumulating capital. Latin American industrial enterprises are not—or at all events are far less effective in doing so. Instead, Latin Americans continually seek capital in the United States or Europe. Very little is said about the fact that they ask that capital from other countries be supplied on terms which they themselves refuse to accept. The education of the Latin American capitalist, it is true, has already begun. But it has much farther to go before Latin America makes full use of the capital which it is forming and can form in its own region.

The foregoing reasons reach their full impact when applied to the problem of securing capital in the public sector. Money expended to build roads, water systems, bridges, port facilities, airfields, or even normal public utility facilities such as electric-light and power plants, can neither offer nor suggest return comparable to the rate familiarly expected by Latin American capitalists. Such expenditures are normally made by national or local governments in these countries—notably the former—and governments have only three ways of raising this money. They may borrow it. They may levy taxes and accumulate it. Or they may inflate their currency in one form or another—traditionally, by having their central banks loan money to the government entity constructing these projects for budget deficits. The Latin American capitalist (not unintelligently from the purely investment standpoint in view of possible inflation) has little interest in buying the fixed interest, 6 or 7 or 8 per cent bonds of his national government or his municipality. While the extractive industries, many of them foreign-owned, are heavily taxed, if a government seeks to gather capital by taxation falling on the local capitalist, he reacts bitterly against paying—a problem squarely faced by the Conference on the "Alliance for Progress" at Montevideo in July 1961. He has been complacent about inflation as a means of financing this form of capital need, partly because he can escape it by judicious deposits of money abroad, while his investments in property tend to rise in rough proportion to inflation. Naturally, where inflation is a problem, his appetite for any form of fixed interest securities diminishes to zero.

There is nothing novel about the Latin American phase of capitalism. It is almost precisely the phase through which Europe passed a century ago—and it produces almost precisely the same political results. The Socialist movement in Western Europe, culminating in the emergence of communism in 1848, proceeded in part from an economic state of affairs similar to the one described above. There, as in Latin America, capitalism was not seriously modified by the powerful religious and altruistic trend which developed in the United States. The radical-revolutionary current in Latin America closely parallels the rise of the Second International in Europe and the later explosion of European radicalism into the Communist and Fascist movements of the twentieth century. Now, of course, the power politics of the overseas Communist powers enter the picture, somewhat as the power politics of Catholic and Protestant states entered into the sixteenth-century struggles of the Reformation.

As political conflicts are increasingly drawn on economic lines within each of the Latin American countries, the position of the United States has its piquant side. She holds a third position. On the one hand she is opposing a group of Latin American politicians who are preaching or plotting the class war and maintaining that the only way to realize the economic potentialities of the country is to break or eliminate capitalists by the Communist route. On the other hand, she preaches to the Latin American capitalists a doctrine which, to them, appears Socialist if not positively Communist. She says: "Take only a reasonable return on your money. Pay much higher taxes. Do not hold great and idle resources in land, meanwhile paying little or nothing to the state, in expectation of reaping great profit from the unearned increment of value as population grows. Do not take your accumulations in liquid assets and send them abroad to the markets of Paris, London, or New York, or to safekeeping in Swiss banks. The price of safety is appreciation of the modern fact that private capital, and the continued existence of the private capitalist, must be continually justified by increased production, better distribution, and visible evidence that the entire country benefits."

Enlightened statesmen like Pedro Beltrán, until recently Prime Minister of Peru, and President Ydígoras Fuentes of Guatemala, both essentially conservative men, likewise preach this doctrine. Some embattled conservatives react very much as the New York financial community reacted when, in 1934, the Congress of the United States enacted the Social Security and the Securities and Exchange legislation. To the extreme left, of course, any doctrine contemplating continued existence of a private capitalist class is "imperialist," "colonialist," and so forth through the whole string of epithets. Yet, one notes, their sentiments do not prevent politicians either of the extreme right or of the left from bombarding Washington with requests for loans, gifts, grants, or other funds, and from asserting that there is a "duty" resting on the United States to produce capital "without strings."

So far as the United States is concerned, all requests could be answered readily enough by simple statement of the conditions under which U.S. funds would be made available, as private banks and private investors state the conditions under which they are prepared to make investments in foreign countries. Contention is sometimes made that to state such conditions is either "insulting" or "economic aggression" or "imperialism." Some Americans even have been absurd enough to take this sort of talk seriously, though Latin Americans do not even expect it to be taken seriously. Yet a deeper problem is reflected. Behind all this farrago of politics and surface talk there are many, many millions of Latin Americans who are entitled to entry into twentieth-century life and to a rising standard of material well-being. Irrespective of politics, the problem is how to connect North American and Latin American resources with them, so that they gain both benefit and awareness of benefit.

At this point, the so-called "democratic parties" become of first importance. The language of modern American democratic capitalism—if capitalism it can be called, for it bears little relation to the type of capitalism found in much of Latin America—is essentially the language of the active political parties whose major concerns are representative government and social reform. Their combined vote unquestionably represents a majority of politically conscious Latin Americans today. These parties would seem reasonably conservative in the United States. But in Latin American context many of them rank left of center. Rejecting both the reaction of the extreme right and the ferocity of the extreme left, these parties represent the real hope of effecting Latin American evolution without undergoing the ghastly experience of a generation of bloodshed, terror, civil war, exhaustion, and eventual reconstruction.

The Alliance for Progress in effect outlined a program of evolutionary reform, acting through economic reconstruction, redistribution of national income, widening of markets, growth in production, and enhanced opportunity for the entire population. It also represented an offer of capital assistance equaled in history only by the capital assistance extended by the United States to Europe through the Marshall Plan. But one of its effects was to frighten local capital and local capitalists, who, it suggested, must contribute—perhaps must even sacrifice. Coupled with cold war dangers and local situations, one reaction has been a limited movement of capital flight.

Whenever such a movement takes place, though it may not last long, American policy must take account of it. If, for every million dollars that flows into Latin America through the Inter-American Development Bank and the AID program, a million dollars is withdrawn by Latin American capitalists, the Alliance for Progress offers little immediate chance of success. If the principle of evolutionary reform were abandoned, the chief result of aid through the Alliance for Progress would be to make a rich Latin American class richer, increasing aggregate productivity somewhat but piling up the returns in the hands of a tiny group. That road would end in an explosion.

The United States has never recommended that Latin American governments take drastic measures to prevent capital flight. This is partly a matter of principle, but perhaps more importantly a realization that exchange controls and control of capital movements are difficult economic operations requiring a high degree of administrative skill and reliability—higher, in fact, than is generally possessed by the countries which may need them most. The United States can, therefore, merely present the problem, and guide her policy according to the capacity with which the social-political organisms of the various countries find themselves able to cope with it.

Foreign Exchange, Foreign Ownership, Foreign Aid

Parallel with the problems of capital accumulation and capital flight, there is a continuing problem of foreign exchange. This enters the picture when capital is sought or provided from abroad, chiefly from the United States.

Because most (if not all) Latin American countries do not manufacture adequately for their own needs, and have not developed adequate sources of energy (coal, oil, electricity) within their own boundaries, they must import a substantial part of their requirements for consumption or development or both. This means that they must develop a high volume of foreign exchange through exports to pay for these imports.

A country like Chile, for example, which imports more than 70 per cent of its manufacturing needs must necessarily export a substantial volume of local products to meet its foreign bills. Chile is an extreme case; in less degree of intensity the problem exists everywhere. So there is powerful motive to "industrialize" and manufacture locally, and also to increase sales in foreign markets. Failure to export to balance needed imports automatically means that the value of the currency of the country, in international exchange, tends to go down. This means that in internal currency the price of imports rises, hardship increases, and eventually imports stop because they cannot be paid for. Therefore, every Latin American political leader blessed with elementary intelligence is constantly thinking of two things: Can he assure continued exports, at a satisfactory price? To relieve himself of that necessity, how can he induce continually greater volume of manufactures ("industrialization") in his own country, and with greater assurance that the profits from such manufactures will stay within the country?

But to increase manufacturing capacity requires capital, and also more foreign exchange. Capital conceivably may be found within the country, provided either by local investors or by the government. Yet if capital must (as is usually the case) be expended to buy foreign machinery and technical assistance, added supply of foreign exchange is needed. Unless it can be provided by selling more local products abroad (which is not always practical), it must be got through foreign loans to, or by foreign private investments in, the Latin American country. Equity investment especially is supposed to be made by private enterprise. A private American businessman asked to invest in those enterprises is apt to ask three questions: By helping industrialization in Latin America, am I not cutting out my own export market? Can I not manufacture more cheaply in the United States? Or, if I invest in local plants, can I get my capital and profits converted into dollars and out in a foreseeable time? He need not be too concerned about his own export market. That market is limited by the amount of foreign exchange available to the Latin American country for its imports. Quite likely he can manufacture more cheaply in the United States. But if the Latin American country has not dollar exchange enough to buy his product, his exports will stop when the exchange runs out.

"Nationalism" in the sense of insistence on building local industries has a sound economic basis—up to a point. The swing point is not discussed by Latin Americans, perhaps because it has not been clearly and definitively thought out and stated either by the U.S. businessman or by his government. It turns on whether the product of the national plant is designed for internal consumption or for export. Operations in a Latin American country whose produce is designed for export, especially to the United States, need more than the mine or oil field, the factory, the smelter or the organization of production, which can be locally provided. They need access to the North American market. Almost invariably that access is best provided, often can only be provided, by an American company. This company may own and operate the local production, or it may work in close relation or partnership with the Latin American enterprise (represented either by its government or, as its social system dictates, by its private businessmen). The local enterprise without the U.S. marketing facility would have rough going. In the Caribbean countries and Ecuador the United Fruit Company, to take a specific instance, produced bananas and other products primarily for export to the United States. It maintained a market in the United States which none of these countries or their nationals could have arranged, especially under free market competitive conditions. Breaking up the United Fruit Company may have been quite justified from the point of view of the antitrust division of the Department of Justice. But it proved damaging to countries like Costa Rica and Honduras, which needed a firm market for fruit. Eliminating the American partner as a rule kills the enterprise.

A greater problem derives from the more emotional and quite understandable feeling of Latin American nations that ownership and control of the industries and chief economic activities of their countries should be in their own hands. This feeling would exist in any case. It is the emotion most citizens of the United States would feel if they discovered that, let us say, most of the American steel industry was owned or controlled in Japan or Germany. Just that emotion indeed did emerge in the United States when at the close of World War I it was discovered that most American radio communication was owned or controlled by the British and the Marconi interests.

That kind of situation lends itself to exploitation by anti-American or Communist propaganda. The word "colonialism" is applied to it by Communist agitators—"Do not American boards of directors settle what happens in our country?" The honest non-Communist nationalist wants to have the American interest, or much of it, sold on negotiated terms to local interests—governmental or private. The Communist agitator ("nationalism" is a standard cover for crypto-Communists) wants to fan anti-American sentiment, hoping to create a situation in which the American interests can be confiscated outright—as occurred in Cuba. Of course he has larger plans in mind: having got that far, he means to confiscate all private property, destroy the upper class, and convert his country into an enemy of the United States and an ally of the overseas Communist powers.

Latin American economists, politicians, and diplomats thus approach industrialization of their countries, through or with the help of American business, with split emotions. Industrialization they want very badly indeed—as they should. They believe (often wrongly) that their respective countries have not capital sufficient to do this, and (often rightly) that foreign exchange will be needed beyond readily available supply. Therefore, they seek U.S. capital. But they also seek arrangements by which ownership and control of the resulting enterprises will be in the hands of their government or their own nationals. Untrammeled U.S. investment in Latin America, even in a political climate encouraging such investment, can lead to an unacceptable degree of ownership of Latin American production by the United States.

This has occurred already in some of the smaller countries. Wholly sincere friends of the United States in Central America often describe the United Fruit Company as "a whale in our pond." Many Chileans have a similar feeling about the predominantly American ownership of their copper and mineral resources. True, neither the great fruit development in Central America nor the exploration of Chile's copper deposits would have occurred save at the initiative and presumably under the ownership of foreign capital—U.S. capital, in fact, since the product was chiefly to be marketed here. There is little dispute that the economy both of Central America and of Chile was benefited by this investment. There is no doubt whatever that the pay and conditions of the workmen in the American-controlled enterprises were substantially better than pay and conditions maintained by Chileans and Central Americans. Disappearance of the foreign enterprises, and of access to markets in the United States on which they depend, would disrupt the economy of the region. The demagogue's or Communist's remedy of "nationalization" offers no solution. A government can confiscate local plantations, mines, or plants. But it does not thereby acquire the market for their product in the United States which makes many such enterprises viable.

None of these facts alleviates the unhappy feeling of Latin Americans aware that essential economic functions in their countries are owned or controlled by foreigners. With a few notable exceptions, American companies owning Latin American enterprises have not seriously sought to work out solutions based on joint ownership, local and North American. One day, perhaps under international plans like that of the European Coal and Steel Community, markets in the United States and production in Latin American countries will be joined in common organization without doing violence to the basic sovereignty of either. But possibilities of this sort of organization have not yet been scratched.

The political-economic fact appears to be that a little foreign investment in a country is welcome, a larger proportion is tolerated, an unduly large proportion is actively resented. Honest Latin American statesmen serving their countries know this and guide themselves accordingly. Large countries like Mexico, Brazil, and Argentina can accept a good deal precisely because of their size. The more rapidly they develop themselves, the more foreign investment they can accept. But beyond a certain limit, prudence for American business and American diplomacy and the political interest of the Latin American governments suggest caution. When the line is approached, foreign investment should increasingly take the form of loans, without attempt to control management. A second limit depends on whether the Latin American country has capacity to export sufficient to provide foreign exchange for the service of her foreign debt. Although some industries may be exceptions, it is a general rule that when both limits have been met, classical movement of capital must stop or at least pause, and a different system has to prevail.

As usual in political controversy, facts as to the results of industrialization through American investment are rarely stated fairly on either side. U.S. business interests point forcefully, and accurately, to the immense development of production in Latin American countries organized and engineered by Americans and paid for by the flow of American investment. Monuments are visible everywhere; and they are impressive. Consequently, American businessmen insist the flow of American investment should be welcomed and encouraged. Latin American statesmen and economists, not to mention extreme nationalists and mere demagogues, object that these enterprises, though they produce, divert the current of Latin American wealth to the United States through profits, growing interest obligations, and repayments of capital. In political controversy, this is called "exploitation." Often it is claimed that the profits of a few years' operations amortize the investment, after which the American company is in position to drain off the subsequent profits in perpetuity.

As there is truth in the contention of the American businessman, there is also a modicum of truth in the Latin American charge. A study prepared by the United Nations in 1955, reviewing the long history of the flow of capital from the United States to Latin America, came to the conclusion that, at that time, the "tendency of investment income paid abroad (i.e., from Latin America to the United States) to exceed the inflow of capital has become more pronounced in recent years. . . . In 1952 . . . the margin between the inflow of private and public capital from the United States and the payment of investment income to that country was $336 million." [2]

While its results were admittedly inconclusive, the study raised doubt as to the capacity of many Latin American countries to absorb more foreign capital on commercial terms. It noted that

[2] U.N. Department of Economic and Social Affairs, *Foreign Capital in Latin America*, E/CN.12/360 (New York: Author, 1955), p. 15.

from 1946 to 1951 the capital outflow from the United States had been $1,629,000,000. But the income received by the United States (on all U.S. capital invested in the region) was $3,078,000,000.

When Latin Americans insist that private investment costs them more in foreign exchange through remittance of profits than it brings in through inflowing investment of capital, they are frequently right.

They are wrong, however, in believing and insisting that these profits are exaggerated or outrageous. The above-cited United Nations study compared the return received on U.S. capital invested in Latin America and on capital invested in the United States itself. Taking a four-year sample when profits were very good (1948 to 1951), the conclusion was that the annual ratio of earnings on Latin American investments to equity varied from 22.2 per cent (a very good year) to 14.9 per cent, and most of this was not sent back to the United States. For the same years in the United States the earnings ratio varied from 13.6 per cent to 11.0 per cent. In some years, in fact, investment in the United States worked out more profitably than investment in Latin America. [3] Average return for the same four years on investment in Latin America worked out at 18.6 per cent; in the United States, 12.4 per cent. Given the added risk, the difference is not out of line. The cry that American companies make and pay out 200 per cent or 300 per cent a year on their investment (familiarly heard on Latin American political platforms) may be dismissed as demagogy. Meanwhile, one could observe that most Latin American investors in their own local enterprises would consider a return of 18.5 per cent on an equity investment scarcely sufficient to make the enterprise worth their while.

Demagogy aside, sympathy must be accorded the many sincere and patriotic Latin American statesmen who, to keep their countries moving ahead, must continually be seeking more capital inflow. To keep their foreign-exchange rates in shape they must constantly devise stratagems to minimize outflow of funds. Up to a point they can provide exchange to remit payments on loans or investments (over and above new capital invested) by ex-

[3] Same, Table 23.

porting the agricultural products or raw materials their countries produce. But they know, as does everyone else, that they are exporting products whose price fluctuates in foreign markets. And in any case the products they export to obtain exchange are largely developed by the sweat of unskilled labor, that is, the lowest paid and least productive labor they have.

Latin American political leaders develop various ways of dealing with this state of affairs. One is simply to let American private investment diminish in those countries which have reached or passed their capacity to absorb it or find foreign exchange with which to pay interest or remit profits. But then if nothing more happens, the rising population of the country, its greater needs for industrial products, and its greater expectations for a rising standard of living will eventually reach an explosion point. Unless, to be sure, the population will supinely accept life under Malthusian conditions of poverty. Another way is imposition of artificial measures to prevent outflow of interest, amortization, or other return on investment. But these almost automatically inhibit inflow of capital, or they precipitate flight of capital already invested and capable of departing. "Nationalization" or confiscation produces the same result with greater speed. Either may satisfy a political outcry at the moment; neither wrestles with the problem. Development must go on; productivity must rise. As we have seen, Latin American productivity has been increasing, but per capita income has not increased at a rate greater than the rising population and social demand, and the increase starts from a fearfully unsatisfactory base.

Latin Americans, although they naturally dislike to admit it, are paying the price for a century of stagnation in their economic and social organization. Emerging from the Spanish and Portuguese empires, from habit they perpetuated colonial methods of management and administration within their now independent countries. For reasons inherent in their history, most of these countries did not have the continuous revolutionary economic movement which modernized the United States. Here, agrarian policy and homesteading began with Jefferson. Monopoly was outlawed after 1890. The United States rationalized banking and taxation after 1912, and systematically distributed the national

income more widely after 1933. Even in the United States none
of these tasks proved politically easy. Now, in Latin America,
when all of them must be done at once, while at the same time
their currencies must be put and kept in reasonable order, the
dilemma of democratic political leaders commands sympathy.
They must convert or fight elements in their own countries whose
privileged position has been hitherto unchallenged. And they
must convert or fight the overt and crypto-Communist agitators
(often paid and armed from abroad) who claim that a single
revolution of class destruction will solve all problems.

Given the political reaction against possible foreign control of
the economy and the economic difficulty in providing foreign
exchange to service a growing debt, if there is to be a large measure of capital inflow from abroad, it must take new forms. They
would have to include grants and "soft loans" either on a govern-
ment-to-government basis or through some central cooperative
organism such as the Inter-American Development Bank. As
growth takes place, of course, the limits of possible action through
more classic channels enlarge.

Within the inter-American system, implemented by the Alliance for Progress, assurance of aid on terms which are not oner-
ous has now been given. The aid is available—conditioned on
honest administration and a valid social use of the capital and
its product.

At the inter-American conference held in Bogotá in the summer
of 1960, agreement was reached for the creation of the Inter-
American Development Bank. On its board of directors sit representatives of all the American republics except Castro's Cuba,
which denounced the scheme as an "imperialist plot" and would
have none of it. Aside from its own relatively small capital funds,
this bank also acts as trustee in the administering of 394 millions
of dollars thus far turned over to it by the government of the
United States, for the purpose of three types of loan. One type,
"hard loans," follows classic lines. Interest and principal are re-
payable in dollars, though on moderate, not to say generous,
terms. The second type, "soft loans," is designed to provide capital for expenditures not likely for a long period of time to produce marketable product, and therefore repayment is arranged

either in the currency of the borrowing country or on terms so long and with interest rate so low that the service of such loans can be no burden. A third type which is likely to be shifted over to the Latin American division of the AID, the new U.S. foreign aid agency, consists of funds really designed as grants for educational and social development wholly noncommercial in character: schools and universities, medical centers, and the like. Finance plus American willingness to assist can bridge the purely economic gap.

Movement of capital of any kind encounters another obstacle which needs frank discussion. This is the capacity of the receiving country to maintain order and organize and administer its affairs generally, and any particular enterprise under discussion, with that degree of honesty and capacity indicating that the resources provided will accomplish a useful result. A government in disorder may not be able even to maintain peace. A corrupt leadership will merely divide the lion's share of the incoming resources among its relatives, friends, and political hangers-on. Latin American politicians can be expert at that sort of thing—it is, indeed, by no means unknown at some political levels in the United States.

Commodities, Prices, Markets

A companion economic problem relates to the price at which Latin American products are sold here. Save in the case of sugar, this problem is almost wholly unsolved. In statistical account, the ratio of price of Latin American exports to the United States (coffee, sugar, cocoa, fruit, copper, lead, and zinc) to the price of imports needed by the Latin American countries will have greater immediate effect on local conditions than any aid program, no matter how spectacular. Here the ultimate source of revenue is the American consumer, whose purchasing power provides the money. By running up the price on any of these commodities in the United States, the individual gain of the Latin American producer is increased. So also is the revenue of his government and the country's supply of dollar exchange. Conversely, a price fall means both individual distress and lessened ability of the government to handle its fiscal affairs.

Latin American governments therefore constantly and quite naturally seek "stabilization" agreements, to maintain prices on an acceptable and a more or less even level. The United States has been slow to enter such agreements, the notable exception being the quota system established by the Sugar Act of 1934, most recently extended for a year in 1961. This act limits the amount of foreign-produced sugar admitted into the United States. The limitation is such that, taken together with domestic beet and cane sugar production, American buyers of sugar pay a higher price than do buyers elsewhere in the world. Through limitation of supply, the American price for sugar remains consistently above the "world price." Admission to this market thus is an immensely valuable privilege, sought with urgency and sometimes undiplomatic bitterness—considering that such admission is strictly a prerogative of the United States.

No similar arrangements exist to stabilize the price of coffee, or cocoa, or fruit—though copper prices have frequently been temporarily stabilized through buying for the U.S. government stockpile and other similar action designed to assist Chile. In the past year, moreover, the traditional attitude of the United States has changed and is now favorable toward stabilization arrangements. But price stabilization, with its obvious attractions, also has its difficulties, practical as well as theoretical. Its advantages chiefly accrue to already wealthy local producers—sugar mill owners, coffee plantation owners, and the like. The benefits may or may not trickle down in great volume to the sectors of Latin American population most in need of the rise in income. Few Latin American governments have maintained tax policies and enforcement of them assuring that the government gets a major share of the profits resulting from increased price, while responsible labor organization in Latin America is still in its infancy. Where taxation has given government a share, Latin American governments have not always made good use of the resources. For example, the "partnership" agreement by which foreign oil companies in Venezuela share their profits with the state (the current rate works out to nearly 70 per cent as the Venezuelan government's share) was in effect through the dictatorship of Pérez Jiménez. The profligate use he made of such of the enormous revenue as did not flow directly into the private fortunes of himself and his adherents can be seen all over the city of Caracas. Finally, price stabilization agreements can be defeated unless, simultaneously, real steps are taken to adjust production to demand. Limitation of production is an extremely difficult problem —as witness the present stockpiles of wheat in the United States.

Accurately apprehended, the problem overpasses economics. It is a question of social organization. Price stabilization seems essential if the Latin American economies are to have a base stable enough to permit development of coherent policy. A deep drop in the price of coffee, for example, could more than counterbalance any sums received by way of aid. But stabilization will lack effect unless adequate limitation of production can also be achieved. And it will lack usefulness unless the benefits to the Latin American exporting country can be distributed in major part to or for the benefit of the workers, who need them most.

In the long pull, there is every likelihood that Latin America, or at least great parts of it, will achieve a common market. Some of the governments have already begun to talk seriously about it, and the Central American countries have already begun to move toward one of their own. As that trend develops—and it may speed up suddenly and decisively as it did in Europe, although the parallel is not a close one—some of the pressing problems of today may be easier of solution.

Inevitably such a market must lead to greater political unity among the member countries. In the long run it should bring a single banking, credit, and currency system, which means, of course, sacrifice of one of the prized privileges of sovereignty—the right and power of a sovereign government to inflate its currency. No Latin American country has really been prepared as yet to make that sacrifice. All have joined the International Monetary Fund under agreements which in theory subject them to a financial discipline tending to minimize inflation and control inflationary policies. But political resistance has been evident; when an I.M.F. commission visited Brazil three years ago, there were even street demonstrations organized against it, though these were probably of covert Communist origin and perhaps need not be taken too seriously. President Quadros, seeking help from the Monetary Fund in April and May of 1961, took the greatest care to make it appear that nothing he did was constrained by his Monetary Fund agreements. He honorably attempted to follow International Monetary Fund recommendations, but he was insistent that the measures he took were solely self-initiated sovereign decisions of Brazil.

Land and Agrarian Reform

Another burning issue in Latin America is that of "agrarian reform." In U.S. official thinking it is accepted that such reform must be encouraged and indeed must take place. But there is a difficulty. In the United States there is only a shadowy understanding of what agrarian reform means, or how it may be brought about.

To begin at the bottom, there is a natural desire on the behalf of every peasant family to own land. This has been true at all times and under all circumstances, and is as true in Latin America today as it was in eighteenth-century France. Simple thinking, therefore, runs toward the idea of expropriating all latifundia, dividing land among the peasants, preferably with some appropriate compensation to former landowners, with assistance to the new owners by government financing, and letting it go at that. The political fact is that except in three countries (Argentina, Chile, Uruguay) more than half the labor force of the country consists of agricultural workers. Land distribution is hopelessly unequal. In Uruguay, where it is "best" distributed, 4.2 per cent of the farm units (or farm owners if you wish) control 56.4 per cent of the land. The next "best distributed" land system is that of Brazil—there, 1.6 per cent of farm units control 51 per cent of the land under cultivation. In other countries, it is worse. This makes a prima facie political and social case for some sort of land redistribution.

The economic case is not so good. Like him or lump him, the *latifundiario* does contribute something. Under his management the land produces more per man and per acre than it does in the hands of the small farmer. When, after 1917, Mexico expropriated about twenty million acres of land and turned them over to some 783,000 peasants under a system of communal ownership (local districts owned in common called *ejidos*), the immediate result was a sharp drop in productivity. When in 1953 the Socialist government of Bolivia did the same thing, farm output fell by an estimated one-third. The United States stepped in then to appease the hunger of Bolivians by making available some of our agricultural surpluses of corn and wheat. Something more is needed than mere cutting up of big estates into small properties. But what is the something?

A number of experiments have been carried out to discover what the missing element might be. By a combination of technical advice, supervised credit, and central technical service (including development of better seed and of agricultural machinery), it appears that needed local organization may be built up. One of the Rockefeller Brothers' experiments with supervised credit and technical assistance was able so to help a group of small farmers in Brazil that their product vastly increased. The International Cooperation Administration of the United States conducted a similar credit and technical assistance program in the highlands of Peru. Perhaps the most dramatic was the program on land utilization carried out by the Rockefeller Foundation, designed to make Mexico self-sufficient in corn—a program which cost a surprisingly small amount of money (not over $5 million), but which drew heavily on technical and agricultural assistance and on the sheer devotion of a group of Mexicans organized and inspired through the efforts of Dr. J. G. Harrar, the present president of the Foundation. When the Mexican administrator of this program died, a day of national mourning was decreed.

Changing the relationships between men and land is a complex process in any event. Reform will differ from country to country, taking into account different ethnic, social and economic conditions and habits, including many elements. To mention one simple factor: water. In the northeast of Brazil and on the west coast of South America (not to mention other areas), land means little without water. Often, systems of irrigation will be needed before the land is worth dividing. The economic success of the Inca civilization in Peru was due to its fantastic irrigation net, now lost but in its time making the western Andes slope a vast, terraced, productive garden.

Marketing will require not only roads but financially responsible cooperatives or their equivalent. Too often now the small farmer is at the mercy of money-lending middlemen who wind up with the lion's share of his crop proceeds and, in time, with his land as well. Usually working with mercantile houses in the market city, they often collect usurious interest rates for crop loans, demand and get as "security" the right to sell the farmer's crop at the lender's own price (or to buy it themselves if advantageous). Small land-owning farmers often are almost as badly off as peons on the great estates.

In these illustrations one fact is clear. More is involved than merely changing the incidence of land tenure. Reform must include setting up new relationships (a) between the farmer and his land and his market; (b) between the man and his land and the technical capacity to get good use out of it (seed, machinery, fertilizer, water, etc.); and (c) between the man and his land and the credit resources permitting him to use the new techniques. "Agrarian reform" means nothing except in a socio-political context. That context will differ from one Latin American country to another. Mexico endeavored to build, with moderate success, on the ancient communal village organization coming down from the Aztec Indian days, which indeed had been protected by Spanish colonial law. Bolivia, still in the throes of revolution, is attempting to do somewhat the same thing, though she has not yet built the context within which the Indian villages, now replacing the old hacienda owners, formerly made themselves effective.

The agrarian reform law in effect in the state of São Paulo, Brazil, worked out by José Bonifacio Nogueira, more nearly reflects U.S. methods; so also does the agrarian law in effect in Venezuela. Long-term credit for the purchase of land itself and cooperative credit facilities for crop expenses are made available, and cooperative marketing of product is envisaged. Also, facilities for education and village services are to be provided by the government.

Probably there will be a good deal of modification in any scheme adopted anywhere, just as there were modifications in the Agricultural Adjustment Act, the Farm Credit Administration, and other measures passed by the United States in 1933. The

United States, favoring agrarian reform through the program of the Alliance for Progress, can hardly claim to have all the answers, certainly not for all the countries in the region, especially when powerful forces within some of them are hostile to the whole idea.

The emotional content of all the talk of land reform is unjust to a good many Latin American landowners. One thinks of the elaborate, painstaking, expensive, and time-consuming effort made by certain great families (the writer thinks of one such in Brazil and another in Ecuador) to work out precisely such contexts with the aid of the state where they could get it, and with their private resources where they could not. There is a great deal more of this than we know about, for the fact is that from 1940 to 1960 the output of Latin American agriculture did increase by nearly 60 per cent.

To pursue cliché iconoclasm once more, it is open to question whether the great "agrarian reform" issue is of as much interest as supposed to the immense majority of agrarian workers (overwhelmingly tenants) of Latin America. It is at least arguable that it is an issue urged primarily by intellectuals and politicians, extending to agrarian workers only gradually, rather than an issue engendered by incipient agrarian revolt. Political forces nevertheless, agrarian or not, are sufficiently interested in agrarian reform so that the problem has to be met; and, humanly, in any case it ought to be met. If the Alliance for Progress and the Conference at Montevideo in 1961 did nothing else, they forced the issue in every Latin American government and will compel all or at least most of them to come up with a projected answer. While it appears untrue that population is now outrunning the food supply, it is equally evident that the food supply must increase with the rapid rise in population that lies ahead—and that most of the people at present are underfed and will use their first increases in income for food. During the early years of his second term as president of Costa Rica, José A. Figueres did succeed in increasing and better distributing the national income and productivity. In the first years the bulk of the increased income went directly into food consumed by the Costa

Rican people. Later, as they were better fed, they used more of their increment for other purposes.

Even a brief review highlights the dilemmas implied in agrarian reform. Peasants want land. Division of land does not produce food. To the contrary, the breakup of the cultivated large estates means, initially at least, a drop in productivity. If distribution is made of unused land—the solution adopted in Venezuela and São Paulo—the dilemma is eased. Though this initially satisfies peasant demands, it does not mean, immediately, more production of food. Nor, of course, does it satisfy the extreme left and its "front" allies. They intend to destroy the landowning classes regardless of economic consequences; to them, no solution leaving them in existence is acceptable. Settlement of peasants on unused land means little unless the new settlers are equipped with a grubstake to enable them to survive the first year of clearing and reducing the land to tillable form, and also a kit of tools or credit by which these can be bought. If the new settlements are to be more than bare and miserable subsistence communities, there must be road connection to cities and markets, schools, water, and a modicum of public utilities. Filling these needs places a financial burden on the state in any case heavy, though it varies depending on conditions. These elementary expenditures have already been made by the large landowners in connection with their productive properties. This fact makes it easy for demagogues to assert that they should be dispossessed, giving the poor the immediate advantage of those past expenditures which give the larger and productive agricultural enterprises their value.

To complicate the question still further, it must be noted that a greater dilemma lies ahead. The ideal of every sincere agrarian reformer is to produce a situation something like that in the United States, where on a relatively small farm a family cannot only live but live in comfort. An American Middle Western farmer is able to do this because, in addition to his land, he has and can use $30,000 worth (or more) of machinery, buildings, and equipment. Fitting out families in this fashion would involve a staggering expense to any Latin American government. Further, few Latin American families understand the use of such equipment and the companion farming methods required. Years of training and experience must be provided. Few Latin American states are presently prepared to give this on a large scale. There have been experimental efforts, sometimes with brilliant results, in Brazil, Colombia, Ecuador, and other countries. But they have not penetrated widely the Latin American consciousness.

Communist dogma here offers no solution whatever. Outstanding in literally all Communist countries is the fact (admitted even by Khrushchev) that they have been unable to solve their agricultural problems. They do not intend division of land, save as a talking-point. After using the argument of land reform to dispose of a landowning class, their next move invariably is to force agricultural labor back into state-owned plantations. At best the agricultural laborer becomes something like a serf; at worst, as in the Chinese communes, he is almost a slave. But this has not increased production, even where (as in China) food is a bitter necessity. In mid-Europe and the Soviet Union, what were granaries for the world before the Communist regimes are now little more than self-sufficient, leaving the less favored agricultural regions under Communist rule in difficulty. Cuba under Castro is following the same pattern. Even in a well-endowed agricultural country like the Soviet Union, Khrushchev seeks remedy in state enterprises for clearing and tilling marginal land, a scheme which has just registered its second successive crop failure. Communism thus offers in Latin America solutions creating conditions worse than those now existing. But left-wing intellectuals in Latin America do not know that, or at least do not advertise it.

Most difficult of all is the problem propounded if and when "agrarian reform" really becomes successful. As noted, 70 per cent of the two hundred million of Latin America's population are employed in agriculture. Compare this with the United States, where 10 per cent of the population produces a greater agricultural product than the country can use. If even fractionally successful, sound agrarian reform means that continually fewer farms and farmers will increasingly and continually produce more and more agricultural product. Over a long pull, this simply means that less and less agricultural labor, employed or self-employed, will be needed. Increasingly there will be excess population in the rural regions. This population will float toward the great city centers—as indeed it is doing now. Many South American cities—one thinks immediately of Rio de Janeiro, Lima, Caracas—are already surrounded with shanty towns and worse, to which surplus agricultural families have migrated to try their luck. Their physical conditions are perhaps not materially worse than those they have left. But they are unemployed and unskilled. Even if skilled, there is not enough industrial employment for them. They eke out precarious existence as best they can, and the areas where they live are often festering sores, even after discounting current exaggeration of these conditions.

Nobody has yet come up with an adequate solution. Latin American cities only gradually develop into the kind of urbanized areas, familiar in the United States, which supply their own balance, solution, and opportunity, as pointed out by Jean Gottmann in his recent study, *Megalopolis*.[4]

Obviously the answer lies in far greater industrialization, when growing employment would, as in the United States, pick up the migrants from the country to the city or, better, to a decentralized group of cities. This indeed is one of the powerful drives behind the Latin American desire for industrialization, requiring a measure of noncommercial movement of capital—one of the fundamental motives which inspired the Alliance for Progress.

Agrarian reform, in the writer's view, must thus take place in the context of a balanced solution. The families offered land must also be offered training, equipment, roads, schools, and public utilities. As the productivity thus created will displace a growing proportion of agricultural labor, urban industrialization must offer jobs. Then, as the whole level rises, the demand for food will rise more than proportionately to the population growth. In any case, actual readjustment will take at least a generation.

[4] *Megalopolis: The Urbanized Northeastern Seaboard of the United States* (New York: Twentieth Century Fund, 1961).

Chapter IV

Education and Information

Although it attracts far less attention, the state of education in Latin America may be as significant as the rate of economic growth. Its main elements must therefore be mentioned before we consider the pressing political questions to which they form a critical part of the social background.

The basic facts of the Latin American educational scene were developed in a report to UNESCO in 1959 and were briefly analyzed by the Research and Policy Committee of the Committee for Economic Development in 1961.[1] For the whole region they presented a shocking situation, though some countries stood out as having achieved notable accomplishment. Taking the United States as comparative base, they showed:

First, whereas in the United States 7.3 per cent of male adults (twenty-five years of age and over) had completed higher education—that is, had some kind of college degree—the next highest country in the hemisphere is Chile where 3.4 per cent had completed such education. Next after that comes Costa Rica with 2.0 per cent, and Venezuela with 1.7 per cent. Then Argentina, Brazil, and Panama with 1.4 per cent each. In the other countries, around 1 per cent of the adult males have college degrees, though some are well below that—Honduras with 0.3 per cent, the Dominican Republic with 0.2 per cent, and Haiti with 0.1 per cent. In aggregate the picture presents a terrible deficiency of men well trained enough to assume the responsibilities of leadership—and

[1] UNESCO, *Basic Facts and Figures, 1959* (Paris: Author, 1960); Committee for Economic Development, *Cooperation for Progress in Latin America* (New York: Author, 1961), pp. 23-25.

higher education in Latin America almost automatically places a man in an elite position.

The situation in secondary education is almost as bad. Whereas in the United States 25 per cent of the male population over twenty-five has completed at least high school education, in Latin America there are only two outstanding countries: Chile with 19 per cent, followed at long distance by Panama with not quite 6 per cent. The other countries run from a low of 0.4 per cent in the Dominican Republic to a high of 4 per cent in Colombia. The average runs about 3 per cent of men with high school training.

As might be expected, the most frightening figures are those showing the percentage of population which has *less* than primary education. In the United States there are 12 per cent in that condition. As might be expected, Chile comes next—there, only 21 per cent lack primary education. At the bottom of the scale Haiti shows 92 per cent without primary education, the Dominican Republic 89 per cent, Nicaragua 84 per cent, and even a great and developed country like Brazil shows 78 per cent. A rough estimate of the percentage of illiterates among persons over ten years of age might run over 60 per cent for the entire region; even in Brazil it is over 50 per cent.

These figures carry the picture only up to the early 1950s. Solid advances have been scored since that time, as a UNESCO study compiled in 1960 indicates.[2] But making all allowances and with the best will in the world, the picture is black enough. The Latin American educational process simply is not meeting the need at any point along the line, from primary education through university training. To paraphrase the late David Lloyd George, one cannot meet Class A problems with a population receiving only Class F education. On any analysis the situation reflects a century of failure in most countries—with occasional shining and brilliant exceptions standing out like beacon lights, notably Chile.

The problem of education is manifestly basic in Latin Ameri-

[2] UNESCO, *Basic Facts and Figures, 1960* (Paris: Author, 1961). This 1960 report, however, does not contain data as full as, or wholly comparable to, those cited above from the 1959 report.

can affairs and has been the subject of many separate studies, local and national. A number of governments—for example, Guatemala—have tackled the task with energy and courage. The technical aspects cannot and should not be here reviewed. But certain observations, many of them unhappy, must be made lest the problem be misunderstood.

Save in a few countries—notably Costa Rica—popular education simply has not been achieved. Every Latin American government pays lip service to the ideal of universal literacy, of opportunity for secondary education, and of an adequate university system. Yet, summarizing results, illiteracy is the lot of at least half the occupants of the region, secondary education is available to a small group, usually the best favored, and the universities, available only to a tiny group, are frequently in a precarious and dangerous position.

The Universities

Let us begin invertedly at the top of the pyramid. In general, Latin American universities follow the European model. That is, the students completing secondary education are supposed to have completed approximately the work corresponding in the United States to the end of the freshman year in college. On entering the university, the student chooses a school which four years later graduates him as lawyer, engineer, doctor, or perhaps economist. The pattern follows the ideal of French university education.

Practically all universities are state-supported, though some, especially those maintained and supported by the Catholic Church, enjoy a certain amount of independent income. Like medieval universities, they commonly enjoy "autonomy." This means not only that they are (theoretically) free from state control, but also that they and student organizations in them enjoy immunity from normal civilian policing. Again, the model followed is that of the medieval University of Paris, which had its own police, its own internal courts, and immunity from the royal and prefectorial military and municipal law enforcement. Though generalization cannot be made over twenty-one countries, some quality of this immunity exists in most Latin American countries.

Healthy as is the principle of separation of school from state, it has in a number of cases given rise to a set of abuses which undermine the educational usefulness as well as the effectiveness of many universities. Without desiring to overstress the effect of the cold war and the Communist movement, one cannot touch the university problem without noting its effects. Students were and are regarded by Communist agitators as a mine of human material, and universities as a golden field for organization. Communists did not invent this: politics and agitation among students are an old and well-established tradition. The fact that drawing students into political activity disturbed the normal process of learning has raised no particular objection. Perhaps for that reason, infiltrating, taking over and using student organizations, is normal working procedure in Communist propaganda and political-action campaigns. All degrees of penetration, from minority foothold to complete control of the university, have been achieved in one country or another.

This comes as a shock to North Americans who may enter Latin American universities as visiting professors or lecturers. They suddenly discover that in the name of "democracy" student control has frequently replaced academic control in matters of major educational policy. For example, a small group of university professors from the United States undertook to give courses as exchange teachers in one Latin American university. In marking examinations they failed a number of students for plain lack of work and incapacity to meet reasonable standards. They were requested by a student organization to change these grades—and on refusal were met with a student strike. The incident in one or another form has been repeated many times. This form of pressure is directed against local professors, against university authorities if a favored professor is not appointed or promoted, or against a rector whose ouster is demanded because he is considered inconvenient; or it is sometimes encountered for entirely extraneous reasons. A student strike in one instance crippled the university because the student organization chose to demonstrate against raising local bus fares, in another case because the student group disapproved of the policy of the national government. As always, the hard-core groups are a minority, sometimes a tiny minority. In extreme cases, they are armed. Frequently the organizers are students in name only: they register for a single course, do not take examinations at the end, and repeat the process the following year. Meanwhile they take advantage of their university enrollment and the favored status accorded "students" to carry on political work. Elections in student organizations have become and are regularly reported as political events sometimes of great importance.

In circumstances where this process has gone to great lengths, the educational side of the university, as might be expected, suffers. While most Latin American universities are able to discharge their function, few of them can count on doing so without periodic difficulties while some find it impossible. In effect, the universities are, in greater or less degree, battlegrounds in the ideological war.

Under these difficult conditions a very large number of able and devoted teachers and professors carry on their work, sometimes against obstacles which would make a faculty member of any university in the United States retreat from an apparently impossible task. Around these men frequently gather groups of students whose devotion and loyalty to them is as fierce as the opposition of the Communist cadres. In some cases student organizations, having beaten off an attempt at Communist infiltration, carry on a defense of the university administration with unexampled tenacity. For the Latin American student is anything but stupid; he is vividly aware of what is going on; vividly aware, too, that the battles within the university reflect and foreshadow equally acute stuggles outside.

The causes of the present condition of Latin American universities are various and many of them are thoroughly creditable. The young men and women in the universities are recognized and recognizably idealists; their idealism commands respect and is respected by public opinion: expression of it individually or as a group is considered desirable. The intellectuals who are faculty members are not considered mere expositors; it is assumed they will have a point of view, and, in social matters, plead a cause. For pleading the cause of popular education (among other things) in a political struggle Sarmiento was exiled from Argentina and as an exile found the opportunity to set up a system of popular education in Chile. The university professor and the students who follow him in controversial matters are rather expected to learn from a process of protagonism and antagonism. This indeed was the case in the University of Paris, at least as long ago as Abélard.

It is said, possibly with some truth, that the habit of activism in student life was powerfully increased as a result of the Spanish Civil War of the thirties. Many Spanish Loyalist intellectuals took refuge in Latin America; many of them were hospitably invited to teach in the universities of their host countries; some brought with them the passionate intensity engendered by the Fascist attack upon and seizure of the Spanish government. During some periods of Spanish history, to be a thinking intellectual almost automatically placed a man in the revolutionary category. Again, university life does give a student his first cold bath of appraisal of his surroundings: if civilization produces the desperate social inequities he sees around him, then civilization must be wrong. It is no long step to conclude that he may be appointed by fate to set it right—a task whose complication and difficulty is only later revealed. As in the case of students in the Soviet Union today, there is a desperate desire to make contact with other students, and with the thinking of other countries.

This atmosphere lends itself to exploitation, for good and for evil. Just as the labor movement almost always is drawn into an orbit of current politics, so are student movements. And here some find themselves unknowingly in the hands of professional manipulators, more especially those working for one or another of the Communist empires and supported by the Russian or the Chinese apparatus. One would not, in most ways, have the Latin American student different from what he is; one could not if one would, although older observers sometimes have a natural and agonized desire to protect youth from being used as cannon fodder, manipulated for the single purpose of power politics, or betrayed without their knowledge to ends alien to their idealistic purpose. The Cuban revolution of 1958 was substantially assisted by the students in the University of Havana. Today most of them and their leaders have either died against the firing walls, or are in prison or exile.

Everything considered, the surprise is that the Latin American universities in the past decade have done as well as most of them have. Few impartial observers, nevertheless, would find the present hypertension conducive to good training or the pursuit of deep scholarship, though many professors and students have surmounted the obstacle.

At occasional extremes, there have been examples of attempts to initiate armed rebellion against the government by hard-core cadres belonging to student organizations. In defeat these groups have sometimes sought sanctuary within the university walls, protected against military and police by the doctrine of "autonomy." It is a bold government which breaks through this immunity, though in extreme cases it has been done. When a few months ago a hard-core group of Castro Communists endeavored to cause revolution in Caracas, and, failing, retired with their Czech arms within the university walls, President Betancourt rightly attempted every expedient before finally permitting the Venezuelan troops to reduce what had become an insurrectionary armed camp. The University of Havana was used by Communist cadres as one base point for the purpose of converting the original Cuban revolution into a Communist revolution in 1959 and 1960. Fortunately, extreme cases of this kind are relatively few, but they have happened often enough to indicate a pattern. Attempts to create it have perhaps been least successful in Brazil and in Costa Rica. In Colombia, fortunate enough to have a number of universities, one or two have been penetrated beyond the danger point, but others have been able to prevent the pattern from emerging at all. Immunity of universities from local police administration does not, obviously, mean immunity from political movements or influence of one sort or another.

Few Latin American professors, unfortunately, are well paid for their academic work; most of them must rely on outside activities or outside sources for additional income. Pressures as well as temptations easily develop from this condition. Finally, since most universities must secure the bulk of their funds from government appropriations, they must make adjustment with the dominant political administration and parties.

The foregoing presents the seamy side of the Latin American university system. Unhappily, the dark as well as the bright side needs to be presented. To a North American a Latin American university with a stately name conjures up a picture of Oxford or the Sorbonne or Bologna—or perhaps of the University of Florida or of California—possibly with a different freight of tradition and excellence. In some cases, the picture is accurate. But by no means necessarily so. The poignant fact is that Latin Americans know the situation, struggle with it, endeavor to reform it—and, when they can afford to do so, frequently send their sons to Europe or to the United States for professional education. The supreme and overriding academic accolade is sought by Latin Americans less in Latin America than in the United States or (most of all) in the universities and academies of continental Europe.

Secondary Schools

Secondary education presents a different picture. It is woefully inadequate because, though its quality is good, the available quantity is so limited that it cannot remotely attempt to give the equivalent of a "gymnasium" education to that stratum of the population which ought to have it. The "colleges" (high schools, roughly equivalent to the French *lycées*) do a remarkably good job of fundamental teaching. A great many of them are private—some frankly undertaken as proprietary schools, some maintained by religious orders. The boy or girl coming out of these schools can read and write his own language and almost invariably one other language, and can do both far better than most high school graduates or even college lower undergraduates in the United States. On the other hand they lead only to professional university training; their graduates who do not go on to this are left without adequate competence for the future, though with enough education to generate discontent.

In spite of—or perhaps because of—their maintenance of classic traditions in educational method and curriculum, graduates of

Latin American *lycées* and colleges are well equipped to tackle university training. But, often being private, their education is too often available only to the more favored economic classes. Change must be noted in this last regard. Until fifteen years ago, good secondary education and university training were reserved almost exclusively for the socially established and well-to-do. Now, the middle classes and the second generation of immigrants who have worked hard and established an economic foothold are appearing in increasing numbers.

Once more, unhappily, we fall under the shadow of the cold war. Recently the Communist propaganda and recruiting apparatus, sometimes directed from a Soviet embassy or other mission, more often from a covert organizing source, has paid increased attention to the secondary schools. Here it has little interest in mass: the recruitment of teenagers and the use of children as arms-bearing cannon fodder, so far as the writer is aware, has appeared only in Cuba. More often, the Communist recruiting agent looks for youths of promise in want of encouragement and in need of help. And help they get, as well as a human attention which they appreciate. As a rule, economic circumstances make them an easy prey. A chosen few are selected for courtesy trips to Moscow or to Communist China and they are meanwhile indoctrinated. They may later be provided with scholarships or assistance during their university years, where they are used to support the infiltration of student organizations. These boys are apt to be able, indeed, are chosen for special attention precisely because they are able. After all, no one else is paying them equivalent attention.

The technique is not new in the hemisphere. In the decade of the 1930s, during the Nazi attempt to infiltrate, powerful use was made of German-staffed secondary schools in which instruction was extremely good—or would have been had the political element been eliminated.

Primary Education and Illiteracy

The problem of illiteracy and primary school education is of formidable proportion. It reflects the greatest single challenge, perhaps, in the entire Latin American picture. All the governments are conscious of it, some have made noble and substantial attempts to wrestle with it. When literacy does not exist in, say, half the adult population, education of adults as well as of children becomes a burning issue.

Some countries have attempted crash programs. Mexico several years ago initiated a campaign calling on every literate person to teach at least one nonliterate person to read and write. Some results were attained though the task was not completely done. More recently the Mexican Minister of Education, Jaime Torres Bodet, has carried out a systematic program whose results command solid respect. Venezuela now provides schools and teachers for every child of primary school age. Castro's Cuba, in December 1961, claimed to have completed a program eliminating illiteracy save among the French-speaking Haitians; there is no way of checking up on the results. Prior regimes in Cuba had, however, paid a great deal of attention to this problem through earlier programs, and the percentage of adult males who had not completed primary education was, relatively, low: 53 per cent, and many of these were not illiterates. The Cuban literacy base was comparatively high. As always, the literacy factor varies from region to region and from place to place depending on the resources and enthusiasm governments and individuals devote to the problem. In Colombia a passionately dedicated Catholic priest, Monsignor Salcedo, who struggles for widespread adult education, using (as means are available to him) radio and television, has scored impressive results.

For the larger future, obviously, primary reliance must be placed not on crash programs (though these are needed) but on basic improvement of the public school systems. These, it must be reported, have been consistently expanding in the past decade. Yet in appraising the advance, weight must be given to the number of children for whom facilities must be provided. Since probably a majority of all Latin Americans is at present under the age of twenty-five, the numbers requiring education must have grown almost as rapidly as have the public education systems.

Trained teachers are far too few in number. By this must not be understood teachers "trained" in accordance with current theories of American teacher training—many of which are scarcely apposite to Latin America. Leaving aside any criticism of these theories, to attempt to train teachers to that extent in the required numbers would be almost impossible at present. The task of a Latin American minister of education is not merely to train teachers for the future—he will want to do that, of course—but meanwhile to make do with what teachers he has and can get, and to secure for them a living wage from the national budget. In that respect his problem is similar to that encountered by the United States seventy years ago, when we took high school graduates and with a modicum of normal-school training made teachers of them—the results were not at all bad. Further, a teacher having a university degree is not attracted to the tiny, desperately isolated villages in the interior; his education and studies, not to mention his ambition, lead him to aspire to and seek a more brilliant career in the great centers.

What Is To Be Done?

The greatest single task of education is to bring great areas of the Latin American region into the twentieth century. Rightly, education has been accorded priority in the program of the Alliance for Progress. Clearly it is not merely a matter of money, though that problem is no mean obstacle in itself. Historically, popular education has been accomplished in original impetus by the drive of men and women inspired by religious or equivalent altruistic motives. Diplomacy, political action, and economic statesmanship can furnish the means. They do not, as a rule, create the sheer devotion required of literally hundreds of thousands of teachers who must dedicate their lives to a career of obscure and unsung local service and whose chief reward has always been, apparently must be, in their own knowledge that they have served well their community, their country, and the generation to come.

This, of course, can and does happen. To such devotion the United States owes the creation of its present public school system, its high literacy, much of its secondary education, and the greatest exemplars of its university system. In like manner, in earlier times the great teaching orders of the Catholic Church laid the foundation for education in Western Europe and Britain. A somewhat similar devotion to Communist ideals provided the base for the solid achievements in this field which the Soviet Union has been able to effect in the past forty years. Latin Americans know the value of inspired and dedicated service in education. We noted the outstanding record of Chile; it is in part the direct result of an impetus given by Sarmiento, whose name glistens perhaps more brilliantly even than those of the liberators and conquistadors.

In more down-to-earth context, the problem of mass education and primary schools presents great difficulty. Systems, unless run by some outside organization—for example, the Catholic Church or Protestant missionaries—tend to come into the political ambit in Latin America as they do in the United States. A schoolteacher's job, though badly paid and arduous, nevertheless is avidly sought after, too often by the less efficient, and peculiarly so in poverty-stricken areas where any kind of job with definite pay is an economic prize worth having. All the problems of political patronage, local control, and desire for the pay rather than the work enter into the scene in Latin America, as indeed they do elsewhere. A great deal can be done merely by maintaining contact with, and honoring, the many existing schools in humble as well as great towns, giving prestige and recognition to good teachers (of whom I have met many) and to educational jobs well done. Latin Americans have no lack of appreciation or sensitivity in this field. Obviously the United States, while it can contribute something, cannot provide the frame or fabric of community anxiety and interest from which good schools come. Still less does diplomacy create a semireligious motivation (the last saint, so far as I know, to come out of a secular foreign office was during the Merovingian era in France). It can merely salute, encourage, recognize, and give a measure of international understanding and significance. The problem of primary education requires not merely impetus from the top of a social-political pyramid downward, but also anxiety, concern, and demand from the bottom up.

That concern exists. Of it there are evidences—spotty perhaps but widespread enough—to suggest that we may be on the eve of

an almost revolutionary demand. True, there are areas in which
no stir is present. Yet a traveler in the backlands repeatedly finds
illiterate fathers and mothers whose greatest desire is to assure
that their children shall learn to read and write, for which they
are prepared to make heroic sacrifice. He finds communities
which recognize that illiteracy is a form of imprisonment preventing either escape or development, which will mobilize their most
meager resources to contribute toward building a school, and
which will revere an old schoolteacher who has become a community heroine.

And one finds local plantation owners, chiefs, and small businessmen who devote endless time to setting up and maintaining
local schools with the help of the local government if they can
get it, without it if they cannot. In the current condemnation of
the "upper classes" presently fashionable, tribute of recognition
must be paid to the many who have accepted this kind of responsibility. The support of one of the great families in El Salvador made possible development of the best medical school in
Central America under the auspices of the national university,
assisted at least one of the secondary schools, and supported primary education on the coffee estates controlled by the family interests. The illustration finds repetition all through the hemisphere just as in nineteenth-century New England local academies were a standard gift to the community by those who had become well-to-do.

Suggestions for American policy have been flowing into the
Department of State and to the administrators of the AID program in some volume. Semiofficial committees, one of them
headed by James A. Perkins, vice-president of the Carnegie Corporation, have been examining university cooperation and the
possibilities for educational effort offered by the AID and Alliance for Progress programs. Presumably some of these efforts will
crystallize into approved projects. One or two suggestions are
worth noting here.

At the university level, former Senator William Benton has
recommended the establishment of one (or perhaps two or three)
private universities completely removed from state control located where political conditions will permit. A few now exist: the

University of the Andes in Colombia and the University of Santa María in Chile are examples. These institutions, presumably free from both political influence and the stormy disputes caused by cold war operations under the banner of "student organization," could devote themselves to education and scholarship. They could and would therefore immediately attain a standing; their degrees would enjoy a respect not accorded to those of institutions in the throes of political struggle; they would immediately attract a constituency of students, teachers, and scholars of first rank. The fact that a degree from the national university is often required for certain kinds of position is an obstacle that would have to be overcome.

Private American foundations have particularly studied possibilities in Central America. There, five small countries (Costa Rica, Nicaragua, Honduras, El Salvador, Guatemala) all maintain national universities. If consolidated into a single Central American university, possibly distributing the technical schools among the five, the ensuing institution would be more powerful, could give better technical education, and could exert a powerful unifying influence on a subregion which has always desired unification. This idea has powerful support in all five countries; conceivably Panama might be added as a sixth. A similar institution might be set up on the Andean plateau. There may be room for a third such institution in Brazil. The Central American project is at present more possible of realization, but other opportunities may open.

Such universities might well become pacesetters for the others. By demonstrating the enormous educational value of removing education from the battlefield of politics, they might stimulate like separation elsewhere. As Senator Benton pointed out, this was the theory on which in the United States the Johns Hopkins University and the University of Chicago were founded.

Secondary schools offer more difficulty, one substantial reason being that they are urgently needed in large numbers. Many of the best secondary schools in a number of countries are at present operated by the Catholic Church or some of its teaching orders; these might be encouraged to organize "branches" or sister schools with local and perhaps international support in their initial phases. Protestants have established and their tradition maintains some notable secondary schools, especially for girls, and these are attended freely by Catholic as well as by Protestant children. Yet in practical possibility the state must be the principal reliance in establishing secondary schools, just as the state must bear the principal burden for primary education.

A great deal of technical work will be needed at all levels: for example, elimination of a nationalism which refuses to recognize the diploma of an accredited school in another country, even extending in some countries to refusal of recognition of degrees in medicine or engineering obtained abroad (this sometimes includes refusal to recognize degrees from the best training schools in the United States). Interuniversity understandings allowing cross-credit for work done could assist at the university level; interprofessional agreements (as for admission to practice of doctors, lawyers, engineers, and other professions) could be worked out—a technical job of some difficulty since the authorities of individual states in the United States are commonly involved. A system of hemispheric accreditation based on quality of training could be of immense service.

Finally, the United States could and must find some method of making the literature of the Western world readily available in quantity in Spanish or Portuguese to Latin America. Surprisingly, books old and new of standard authority in English, French, and German are not freely found in the all-too-few Latin American libraries or in the very numerous Latin American bookstores. These are well stocked with publications originating in Spain and in other countries of Latin America. But the powerful scientific, philosophical, and historical, not to mention technical, literature originating in Western Europe and the United States is relatively unknown and woefully inaccessible. On the other hand, a full collection of Russian literature, especially Marxian, is available everywhere: it has been translated into the language of the country, has been printed and bound in paperbacks, is on sale at nominal prices near every university, and is available at all bookstores. It was recently reported that the Soviet Union had contracted for large-scale publication of the standard Marxist and approved books through the printing presses of Havana, with Latin American distribution handled by the whole propaganda apparatus. Half a generation of literate people in Latin America is scarcely aware that Western education, culture, and scholarship produce either text books, treatises, scholarly studies, or literature. But they can afford and do read the Communist output.

At last count, the government of the United States was spending a little over $100,000 annually toward making American and Western books available to 185 million Latin Americans! The private effort was also unimpressive. This problem, in the view of the writer, should be taken with extreme seriousness. Under present conditions, the Communist apparatus has had the vision and the sense, the energy and the money, virtually to create the literature at all levels on which intellectual life in much of Latin America is increasingly based. There are notable exceptions: Brazil, with an active publishing trade but limited in its ability to secure translation into Portuguese; Colombia, whose literature is flourishing, but again largely limited to books from Spain and Latin America. The writer has often wondered whether money could not be secured for translation and circulation in Latin America of many of the reputable products of the reputable paperbacks now appearing in the United States and in Great Britain, and their sale at prices competitive with the Soviet and Soviet-chosen literature.

* * *

We may end these observations as we began, with an unhappy allusion to the cold war. Soviet strategy has been not only to organize hard cores capable of armed seizure of power, but simultaneously to train a generation of men devoted to Communist principles and designed to be the principal reservoir of human capacity to take over and administer the affairs of the various Latin American countries. The more of these trained men, the more readily possible it becomes to set up, over a period of ten years or so, an exclusively Communist elite. This process is fairly well advanced: the program, though apparently reaching full speed only three or four years ago, is operating in high gear now. Graduating, let us say, one hundred Communist-educated technicians (economists, teachers, scientists, engineers, doctors) every year into the life of a small country whose stratum of well-trained men is narrow at best will over a decade set up a reserve of one thousand men anchored, so far as education can do it, to Leninist thinking—because, indeed, they have had no solid intellectual contact with anything else. The educational poverty of great parts of Latin America makes some of its countries obvious and easy targets. If this be combined with skillful annexation of professors and teachers in the local universities and schools, aided and supported by overt or covert means, the effects rapidly become visible. The "transfer of allegiance of the intellectuals" (Lenin's phrase) goes on apace.

Were this education divorced from the power politics which engender it, one might be philosophical. The United States is under no compulsion to conscript Latin America, or indeed any other countries, into its own peculiarly sophisticated mold which has left both Marx and nineteenth-century capitalism far behind. But at present there is no such divorce. As in the case of the Nazi attack on the hemisphere in the thirties, for the Communists ideology is a means to a power-politics end; and that end is development of a strong local constituency under the control of one or the other of the Communist power centers overseas.

There is, nevertheless, no need to be unduly depressed. Enough evidence exists already to prove that students held within the rigid limitation of Communist training and authoritarian education seek and desire contact with a world outside, whose existence they apprehend but from which they have been cut off. Contact with the stream of Western ideas means liberation as well as education. The cold war is not an insuperable obstacle to education, or to the flow of ideas developed from and impelled by the Western tradition of constant search for objective truth.

Provided, of course, that energy and devotion to the humanist ideal is expended in degree equal to that put forth by its adversaries.

Chapter V

Bases of Inter-American Diplomacy

In the Western Hemisphere the United States holds predominant power, economic and military. So indeed she should. Her population is almost equal to that of all the Latin American states combined. Though she must be considerate of the needs of her neighbors, her first duty, of necessity, is to her own peoples. Her resources, military and economic, must guard them and provide for their needs. This condition will continue to exist during the foreseeable future, though the disparity in favor of the United States will gradually decline as the Latin American states grow in population and economic capacity.

There is nothing illegitimate in the current superior position of the United States. Breast beating or guilt complex, indulged in by some, is merely absurd. The position of the United States, past or present, did not arise from her economic or other relations with Latin America; these have contributed and now contribute only marginally to her economic position. And the condition of Latin America is not the product of the United States, either politically or economically.

The hard-core national interest of the United States can be simply stated. The overriding and continuing interest is the defense of her own country and her own people—just as the first interest of every Latin American state is the defense of its own. No government in the United States or elsewhere in the hemisphere can change that situation.

Unhappily, in the modern world no government can regard defense as beginning only at its geographical borders. A nation unable to defend itself until war crosses its frontier is almost automatically doomed, at least initially, to defeat, and in any case to terrible devastation. This condition also cannot at present be altered. The point at which defense beyond a nation's borders becomes essential differs with conditions and in the outer periphery is always open to some question. Apparently, modern methods of war increase the beyond-border necessities in distance if not in intensity.

These unalterable conditions dictate this hard core of fixed policy for all Western Hemisphere countries. Diplomats of the United States as well as of Latin America have to take account of them because they cannot change them. The United States can make concessions up to the point where these paramount interests are involved. After that, she must set up or maintain conditions of her defense.

The point is here stated forcefully, because the least kindly act possible is to permit any country with which the United States deals to entertain the slightest doubt on the proposition. When in 1939 the defense interest of the United States as against the Nazi-Fascist aggression became clear, the "Good Neighbor" policy could not, did not, and was not expected to prevent the United States taking the necessary economic and military measures to arrange for her defense, even though a number of Latin American governments then flirted with the idea of casting their nations' lot with the Axis powers. Somewhat the same situation obtains in the so-called cold war (which is by no means cold in some Latin American areas) raging today.

The Hemispheric Line

In announcing the Monroe Doctrine on December 2, 1823, the United States tacitly took the view that her outer line of defense was the boundary of the hemisphere. At the time this was a warning to Spain, which sought to reconquer her lost American empire, and to Russia, which sought to colonize the Pacific northwest of North America. Concurred in by Britain out of foreign-policy considerations, this barrier protected the independent existence of the Latin American nations as they came into being and prevented division of South America in the fashion by which Africa was parceled out among European powers during the nineteenth century. A unilateral act, the Monroe Doctrine later encountered resentment among Latin Americans, despite their obvious debt to it. It became, in theory, multilateral at the Buenos Aires Conference of 1936, as a result of the diplomacy of President Roosevelt and Secretary of State Cordell Hull, the conception being that of Sumner Welles. This action assumed that all American states, and not merely the United States, had the same interest. It also assumed that any American state which became a colony of an extra-continental power or entered its political system in form or in fact automatically became unfriendly.

This doctrine, either in the form given it by Monroe or in the inter-American system, has always excited the opposition of overseas aggressors on the march. Kaiser Wilhelm endeavoring to intrigue with Mexico during World War I, Hitler and Mussolini planning their drive for world conquest a generation later, and Chairman Khrushchev in his fulminations of more recent years have all characterized it as obsolete, dead or "dying." The motive in all three cases was a design eventually to destroy the power of the United States. Intent to enter the Western Hemisphere is an announced active element in both Soviet and Chinese policy today. At present the Soviet Union is using the Castro regime in Cuba as its active spearhead. Statements both by Khrushchev and Castro leave no room for rational doubt on the point.

The United States has not changed its ideas. In 1938 President Roosevelt, dealing with the possibility that some Latin American states might fall under the domination of the pro-Axis groups, publicly observed: "Do you think that the United States would stand idly by and have this European menace right on our own borders? Of course not. You could not stand for it. . . . We probably all agree that we could not stand for a foreign nation doing that under the guise of a Mexican flag." [1]

Until today, all Latin American governments (with the current exception of Cuba) have paid lip service to the doctrine that no

[1] *The Public Papers and Addresses of Franklin D. Roosevelt*, 1938 Volume: *The Continuing Struggle for Liberalism* (New York: Macmillan, 1941), pp. 255-256.

American state must fall under the domination of any extra-continental system. How firmly they mean it is another question.

Many of the Latin American countries undoubtedly do mean it. The five Central American countries and Panama, and both Haiti and the Dominican Republic, know perfectly well that their continued independence depends on their defense by the inter-American system or, if that system breaks down, then on defense by the United States. In practice, this means defense by the force of the United States in either case. If cut off from an inter-American system backed by North American force, or, failing that, from the direct support of the United States, their shrift would be short as against any aggressive extra-continental power. They would not even be safe as against each other or against more powerful Latin American states, which from time to time can become as aggressive in a small way as larger powers can be in theirs.

The experience of these small states with the United States has not always been happy. Yet in a century and a half their independence and nationhood have invariably been preserved. Thus it was not accident that every Caribbean state other than Mexico joined the United States at once in 1941 after Pearl Harbor and indeed were the only ones to do so. Other Latin American states wobbled in declaring themselves, though the smaller states in South America proper, probably from like motives, rapidly declared for the United States shortly thereafter. Ecuador, for example, immediately permitted use of the Galápagos Islands for an American naval base. Colombia, more cautious in her declarations, nevertheless promptly moved to assist American defense, as presently did Venezuela. Their statesmen and politicians did not do this on sentimental grounds, nor even because of the declaration of continental solidarity agreed upon at Lima in 1938. They did so because, unless the United States defended herself, they lay naked to any extra-continental warship sailing into their ports. They were, in a word, dependent on the United States and on the then embryo inter-American system to maintain their ultimate national interest in existence.

Elsewhere, the sense of dependence for defense has not been

so clearly seen. Brazil, the largest state, underwent political struggles of some proportion before its public opinion and its then dictator, Getulio Vargas, determined that the ultimate interest of the country lay with the United States. Argentina, the most distant, eventually joined, though in name only. Mexico, singularly detached psychologically, also arrived at a like conclusion though her reasoning is obscure. The early reactions of the Latin American countries in most cases accorded with their appraisal of reality, even in the case of Mexico whose statesmen thoroughly understood that the United States, when under attack, could not accept a hostile or hostilely dominated neighbor on her flank.

"Independence"

The realist base of the diplomacy of the Western Hemisphere in 1962 remains much as it stood in 1938. Now, as then, certain movements in Latin America oppose it, adopt slogans, and endeavor to excite corresponding diplomatic attitudes on the part of their governments and foreign offices. One of these movements proceeds on the slogan of "independence." Since all Latin American nations are sovereign and are as independent as nations can be in a crowded world, word and slogan imply more than they say. "Independence" in this sense is intended by politicians who use it to mean capacity to act contrary to the interests of the United States, though rarely explained thus frankly. It also can be explained as a quite legitimate desire that the government involved shall not be merely a "yes-man" to the United States. The word was used most forcibly by former President Janio Quadros of Brazil. He did not undertake to spell out what he meant in advocating that Brazil pursue an "independent" foreign policy, but suggested its content by reference to Nasser and Tito.

Independence in foreign policy is entirely within both the right and the power of any sovereign state. If the United States maintains diplomatic relations with the Soviet Union, it is difficult to object that Latin American countries should not maintain similar relations. If Great Britain expands her trade relations with the Communist world (as she does), there is no valid reason why the nations of this hemisphere should not market their products behind the iron curtain if they can, or purchase iron curtain goods in return.

Action independent of neighboring states, however, has a powerful corollary. In taking such action governments have to take account of two facts. The first is that they become solely responsible for what they do. The second is that then other governments may, and indeed perhaps must, act independently of them and their interests. Tacit assumption is usually made by most Latin American politicians advocating "independence" that the United States in hemispheric affairs will under all circumstances maintain a policy of cooperation with and consideration for her Latin American neighbors quite irrespective of the line taken by them. There is no reason in international law to prevent any Latin American government's seeking trade relations and accepting economic assistance from the Soviet Union under the program followed by the Soviet government since 1954, or severing itself from the policy of common hemispheric defense. But, equally, there would then be no legal or moral reason why in such cases the United States should not be free to consult her own independent national interest in giving or withholding any aid she may be providing by grant or loan, or in reviewing any measures she may have taken to stabilize or assist markets for her neighbor's products. A double standard of independence is neither possible nor self-respecting.

So far as economics is concerned, since the enunciation of the "Good Neighbor" policy in 1933, the policy of the United States with respect to the Western Hemisphere has not been one of "independence." She has sought to follow a policy of agreed cooperation within a regional family of nations. That policy found expression in the O.A.S. Charter of 1948, Article 63 of which sets up the Inter-American Economic and Social Council for "the promotion of the economic and social welfare of the American nations through effective cooperation for the better utilization of their natural resources, the development of their agriculture and industry and the raising of the standards of living of their peoples." But cooperation can never be a permanent one-way street. Neither by treaty, nor by morality, nor by ordinary common sense is it any state's obligation to cooperate with another state which finds it to its interest to be hostile in essential matters.

Some extremist Latin American politicians, like many politicians in neutralist and underdeveloped countries elsewhere in the world, have developed an illusion that the United States "cannot" withdraw from a policy of economic support. In unexplained fashion, they consider that they, on behalf of their countries, have a "right" to draw on the resources of the United States. When it is pointed out that any time the Congress of the United States, or its public opinion, may simply decide to end such programs, the answer is a sort of incredulous horror. "But you cannot," is repeated over and over again. The more naïve parrot the classic threat: "But then we would go Communist." But cooperation based on fear of that kind is worth little or nothing, and there is plenty of political pressure in the United States to terminate cooperation at once whenever that argument is used.

If "independence" means breaking away from the inter-American system, it automatically implies willingness to take the consequences of withdrawing from that system, possibly on the theory that the blackmail value of the resulting position would be more useful than the advantage of mutual friendship. Outside the inter-American system no Latin American country would have automatic right to participate in the program of the Alliance for Progress or (perhaps no less important) any particular claim to sell her goods in the markets of the United States. The passionate insistence of a number of Latin American countries, and of Brazil in particular, after the Cuban sugar quota had been cut off, that they had a "right" to a portion of the Cuban quota enabling them to sell sugar in the United States at the higher price paid by American consumers was a remarkable exhibition of faith in the inter-American system and in the cooperative attitude of the United States, and at the same time a misunderstanding of the basic situation. For if any one thing is plain it is that preferential access to the American market and the right to sell to American consumers at a price higher than that ruling elsewhere in the world lie solely and peculiarly in the sovereign choice of the United States.

Fairly analyzed, every country in the hemisphere and out of it is and should be wholly independent in dealing with all problems, including the type of political and social structure it desires to have. This right is essentially juridical in its base. In matters of international attitude and policy, though every country has the right to act according to its choice, no government in existence (including the United States) can act without considering policies and countermeasures which others may take, with equally unquestioned juridical right, as their interest may dictate. And in matters involving economic relations the word "independence" is almost meaningless. Economic exchange between countries is bilateral or multilateral; no party is or can be "independent" of that fact. There is, to be sure, the juridical capacity to withdraw from the complex of trade and commerce. But exercise of it is practically impossible to any save primitive communities. Part of the political emotion finding its way into Latin American diplomacy results from awareness of this reality. This is understandable: each of us would like to have the privileges of economic life in a complex world without the attendant burdens, and resents the fact (for which no one is responsible) that the burdens are inevitable.

Noninterference

Classically, in international practice, nations are not expected to assume positions in the internal political affairs of their neighbors. The rule has been honored as much in the breach as in the observance all over the world, but it still holds. The consequence of meddling in internal politics is resentment by the group considering itself politically disadvantaged. Normally, therefore, the foreign offices of the American states, including the United States, do not take positions in respect of the internal political matters of their neighbors.

But in current context the rule becomes extremely difficult to follow. In many, perhaps most, Latin American countries there is a party or group of parties overtly or covertly Communist, whose activities and demonstrations are openly directed against the United States, against her friends, and in favor of one or another of the Communist powers. In practice, the right of the

United States to exist is at present one of the issues in some aspect of nearly every Latin American political campaign. Currently, this sort of local political activity is at a high point. The embassies of the United States cannot ignore this fact and ought not to be expected to. Detachment under those circumstances is impossible.

Any rule of "noninterference" at this point would be strictly a one-way street. The Communist powers, directly or indirectly, spend large sums annually to finance these movements. When it is skillfully done, their embassies or official representatives may not appear overtly involved, although the home governments indulge little restraint in their statements. More often, the local work is done through unofficial agents and through party machinery subservient to their plans. Apparently, perhaps through force of necessity, these activities are taken for granted by most, if not all, Latin American governments. Far from expecting that the United States will refrain from any activity, many Latin Americans insist that the United States ought quite openly to engage in propaganda and other measures to counteract Communist efforts. Many urge that the United States should, discreetly, assist her political friends, pointing out that the Communist powers almost openly finance and assist theirs.

The first point seems well taken. Nominally the United States has not seriously engaged in "propaganda" as such. Her activities are stated to be "informational." Whatever descriptive word is used, there is no adequate reason why the United States should not engage in advocacy with the same vigor as her opponents, especially in view of the fact that she and her policies are the direct subject of attack. Certainly action could be taken to prevent local and private U.S. interests from assisting the nation's overseas enemies. In a number of countries anti-American newspapers have large circulation. American companies use them for advertising media; American advertisers thus help to finance anti-American campaigns. Exactly this condition prevailed in 1939 and 1940 when Nelson Rockefeller, then Coordinator of Inter-American Affairs, worked out the "blacklisting" program which provided that the advertising and trade operations of American concerns should be so handled that they did not pro-

vide revenue and funds for the anti-American Nazi operations.
When later Germany declared war on the United States, the operation was reorganized as economic warfare—a point not yet
reached today.

The principle, plainly, must be that the United States shall
not use either political or economic influence in any internal
matter which does not directly concern her, and which is not
stimulated from outside the country involved. The rule of noninterference must be the prevailing policy. But the policy can
hardly be maintained where the Latin American country is unable
to prevent, or by its protection of free speech cannot inhibit,
extra-continental powers from engaging overtly or covertly in
internal propaganda or campaigns aimed at the United States.
Nor, in fact, do most Latin American governments seriously deny
this.

Engaging in internal party struggles is, of course, another matter. In many Latin American countries the government of the
United States is almost invariably besought by one or another
political group to assist its cause. Especially when such groups
are in opposition it is also asserted that the United States, by
maintaining trade and aid relations with the current government,
in effect assists or supports the government in power. In Latin
America (as in the United States) the party controlling the
government usually benefits politically if the government is able
to carry on construction, public works, and other economic projects. Where these are financed by the United States, the government's opponents frequently make the accusation that the United
States is "involved in internal politics." We may gain some relief
from these charges when much of the financing is done by the
Inter-American Development Bank and similar institutions as
inter-American bodies. The quarrel, if any, is then with an inter-
American body, not with the United States. There will nevertheless be some continuance of the familiar charges: Latin Americans, like North Americans, know that the bulk of the assets of
these institutions comes from this country. But this cannot be
helped, and perhaps the accusations should not be taken too seriously.

On the purely political side there is also an exception to the noninterference rule. In the Charter of the O.A.S. there is a clause (Article 5, d.), which reads as follows: "The solidarity of the American States and the high aims which are sought through it require the political organization of those States on the basis of the effective exercise of representative democracy." Under this clause complaints have been made for a decade against dictatorships, with insistence that the United States should not support them. Normal relations are frequently interpreted as political support, particularly if the dictators are receiving loans or arms under aid agreements. On the other hand, a dictatorship outlawing opposition immediately and necessarily converts any opposition into conspiracy. It tends therefore to assert that any contact anywhere between the U.S. government and opposition elements is "interference" in its internal affairs. The dilemma for American policy is obvious. The United States maintains, as it should, diplomatic relations with all kinds of governments, including dictatorships. Yet the only certain fact about any dictatorship is that it eventually ends. At that time a new government is formed. If the new party succeeding to power has consistently been denied contact with Americans, its resentment is apt to be great. Of interest is the fact that three outstanding Latin American presidents today, President Villeda Morales of Honduras, President Lleras Camargo of Colombia, and President Betancourt of Venezuela, during the period of dictatorship in their countries were in exile or under restraint by the dictators. All were men entitled to the esteem of the hemisphere; all maintained contact with unofficial American groups, though in a number of cases the State Department actively disapproved. There was, in fact, excellent reason why the government of the United States should have favored such contacts.

Obviously, in nondictatorial countries, normal contact should be maintained with the politicians of all parties, opposition as well as government. This indeed is expected, accepted, and standard practice.

A situation is now emerging in which the United States has to deal with powerful animosities between some of the Latin American countries themselves. On December 9, 1961, Fidel Castro in Cuba violently attacked the presidents and governments of Venezuela, Colombia, and Panama in his habitual insulting terms. He concluded by breaking relations with Colombia and Panama (Venezuela had already broken relations because of Cuban complicity in a revolutionary movement against the Venezuelan government). On February 4, 1962, fortified by a message of support from Nikita Khrushchev, he proclaimed from Havana a movement to overthrow governments in fourteen of the twenty countries. Those Latin American governments which still maintain relations with Cuba—Argentina, Brazil, and Mexico among others —will automatically come under Cuban and Soviet diplomatic and propaganda pressure to become hostile to all anti-Castro governments while, of course, political warfare will rage between Cuba and the governments for whose overthrow Castro is calling. There are few precedents and no norms in this situation. To state the fact bluntly, the overseas Communist powers, using Cuba as a spearhead, are seeking to organize and incite Communist rebellions in a number of Latin American countries and intend eventually to do so in all. In a number of cases the rebellions have internal causes, but they may be externally fomented, and the overseas Communist powers make a practice of exploiting internal unrest. There will indeed be attacks on the sovereignty of the countries in question. This campaign will be carried on by the Communist and pro-Communist political parties within those countries supported from outside by whatever resources of money, arms, and propaganda Castro's Cuba or the extra-continental Communist powers can supply.

A "hands off" attitude by the government of the United States in these situations would probably be as gravely misunderstood as a policy that might be condemned by some as "meddling."

Nonintervention

"Nonintervention" is applied both to doctrine and to policy. Doctrinally, it has a quite specific meaning. Until 1933 it was generally considered that a nation having the power could "intervene" in another country to protect its citizens, maintain its rights under international law, and, in an extreme case, put an end to anarchy. By "intervention" is meant use of force within another country, or blockading it. In some cases (Cuba, Haiti, Panama) prevailing treaties gave the United States the right to do exactly this. Secretary of State Charles Evans Hughes stated the proposition at the Havana Conference of 1928: "Now it is a principle of international law that in such case a government is fully justified in taking action—I would call it interposition of a temporary character—for the purpose of protecting the lives and property of its nationals." [2]

Unhappily, it is far easier to put armed forces into a country than to determine their action when they get there, and it requires near genius to get them out. Blockade immediately brings complication with all other countries whose ships, or today aircraft, desire to enter the blockaded area. In this century the United States intervened under its treaty rights in Cuba, in Haiti, in the Dominican Republic, and in Nicaragua. In no case were the results either effective or impressive, and they excited the bitterest hostility in Latin America. This led President Franklin Roosevelt to ponder the possibility of removing from the American republics any fear of aggression, and at the same time moving toward a hemispheric partnership,[3] and to the pledge made by Secretary Cordell Hull at the Conference of Montevideo in 1933 that the United States would no longer resort to intervention. The pledge reached permanent form at the Conference of Buenos Aires in 1936, in a declaration drafted by Luis Manuel Debayle (then Foreign Minister of Nicaragua) and by myself. It reads:

> Article 1. The High Contracting Parties declare inadmissible the intervention of any one of them, directly or indirectly, and for whatever reason, in the internal or external affairs of any other of the Parties.
>
> The violation of the provisions of this Article shall give rise to mutual consultation, with the object of exchanging views and seeking methods of peaceful adjustment.
>
> Article 2. It is agreed that every question concerning the interpretation of the present Additional Protocol, which it has not been possible to settle through diplomatic channels, shall

[2] *Report of the Delegates of the United States of America to the Sixth International Conference of American States, Held at Habana, Cuba, January 16-February 20, 1928* (Washington: GPO, 1928), p. 14.

[3] Memorandum, Roosevelt to Stephen Early, May 17, 1942.

be submitted to the procedure of conciliation provided for in the agreements in force, or to arbitration, or to judicial settlement.[4]

The language of the resolution both then and thereafter was understood by the United States, and for that matter by everyone else present, to mean, quite specifically, the renunciation of intervention as defined in international law. From it came the words of Article 15, the nonintervention provision of the Charter of the O.A.S.

As will later appear, this provision did not modify or abridge the right of any American state to defend itself, or to act under any arrangement for collective defense.

The O.A.S. and Hemisphere Security

The effective documents constituting the inter-American system are two: the Charter of the Organization of American States (familiarly called "The Charter of Bogotá") and the Inter-American Treaty of Reciprocal Assistance ("The Treaty of Rio"). They must be read together. Both were blocked out by the Conference of Chapultepec held in Mexico City in 1945. Preparatory work for both went on simultaneously, the Rio Conference being held in the late summer of 1947 and the Bogotá meeting in the spring of 1948. They cannot be separated, nor do the provisions of the Charter of Bogotá subtract anything from those of the Treaty of Rio.[5]

The Organization of American States is a regional association of nations primarily responsible for maintaining collaboration, adjusting differences, and avoiding war in the Western Hemisphere. Its Charter, signed on May 2, 1948, amid the wreckage

[4] *Report of the Delegation of the United States of America to the Inter-American Conference for the Maintenance of Peace, Buenos Aires, Argentina, December 1-23, 1936* (Washington: GPO, 1937), pp. 127-128.

[5] For texts, see *Inter-American Treaty of Reciprocal Assistance,* signed at Rio de Janeiro, September 2, 1947, in Raymond Dennett and Robert K. Turner, eds., *Documents on American Foreign Relations,* v. 9 (Princeton University Press, for the World Peace Foundation, 1949), pp. 534-540; and *Charter of the Organization of American States,* signed at Bogotá, Colombia, April 30, 1948, in same, v. 10 (1950), pp. 484-502.

of the Bogotá riots gives definite form to a looser organization which, stemming from the Pan American Union, had existed since 1890. Its precise purpose is stated in its first Article:

> The American States establish by this Charter the international organization that they have developed to achieve an order of peace and justice, to promote their solidarity, to strengthen their collaboration, and to defend their sovereignty, their territorial integrity and their independence. Within the United Nations, the Organization of American States is a regional agency.

Its essential objectives are (Article 4):

> a. To strengthen the peace and security of the continent;
> b. To prevent possible causes of difficulties and to ensure the pacific settlement of disputes that may arise among the Member States;
> c. To provide for common action on the part of those States in the event of aggression;
> d. To seek the solution of political, juridical and economic problems that may arise among them; and
> e. To promote, by cooperative action, their economic, social and cultural development.

Article 5 provides, among other things, that the solidarity of the American states "require the political organization of those States on the basis of the effective exercise of representative democracy"; it also provides that an act of aggression against one American state is an act of aggression against all other American states. Article 15 carries forward the nonintervention principle:

> No State or group of States has the right to intervene, directly or indirectly, for any reason whatever, in the internal or external affairs of any other State. The foregoing principle prohibits not only armed force but also any other form of interference or attempted threat against the personality of the State or against its political, economic and cultural elements.

The Organization of American States acts through meetings of its Organ of Consultation, an inter-American conference, or a meeting of the foreign ministers or their representatives. Such a meeting can be convoked on request of any party to the treaty.

Self-defensive action by any party, however, may precede such a meeting; and it may, of course, take place if no meeting is called or held.

The Charter specifically authorized (Article 39) meetings of ministers of foreign affairs to serve as an "Organ of Consultation" —presumably the same sort of meeting referred to in the Treaty of Rio. But under the Treaty of Rio, the Organ of Consultation can only take binding decisions as to measures of collective (not individual) defense by a two-thirds vote, while the Inter-American Conferences or the meetings of foreign ministers (either of which may serve as the Organ of Consultation under the Charter of Bogotá) may act by majority.

There is also, at a lower level than the meetings of foreign ministers, the Council of the O.A.S. This body consists of a representative of each state, with rank of ambassador, sitting at Washington. In result, when any collective action is sought, alternative procedures are possible: (1) A simple meeting of "consultation" of foreign ministers may be convoked by any party; or (2) if defense or threat to peace or security is concerned, a meeting of foreign ministers may be convoked to act as the "Organ of Consultation" under the terms of the Treaty of Rio (in which case a two-thirds vote is required for collective action) or under the terms of the Charter of Bogotá, or (3) a meeting of the Council of the Organization of American States may be held. This third alternative is weaker because it means, essentially, only a meeting of ambassadors. As the arrangement has worked out, the Council has not developed great initiative.

The Treaty of Rio sets up obligations—but no machinery for military action. The Charter of Bogotá provided for an Advisory Defense Committee "on problems of military cooperation." But this committee was never organized, and military matters have been handled by the Inter-American Defense Board, an advisory and consultative body dating from the period of wartime cooperation. Every American state has a right to be represented on that board, a fact which leads to strange anomalies. Prior to the Punta del Este Conference of 1962, Castro's Cuba, though cooperating closely with overseas Communist powers and having as a stated objective the overthrow of all the other American countries and breakup of the inter-American system, had a representative on the Defense Board. Naturally, many of the other American states were not particularly interested in discussing measures for their own defense against extra-continental powers in the presence of the representative of a satellite of the very powers against whom these measures are most likely to be taken. There were ways of circumventing that obstacle—the brilliant young Ambassador Carlos Urrutia of Guatemala has pointed out and used some of them with great astuteness. But the entire scheme assumed unanimity of all parties in the interest of defending the American hemisphere and excluding extra-continental powers from participation in its affairs. This unanimity no longer existed. Only the expulsion of the Castro regime from the inter-American system after Punta del Este made it possible to restore it.

U.S. policy has been, without waiving its individual rights, where possible to seek approval of any action in respect of the defense of Latin America, or of any individual Latin American country, by the Organization of American States. Until recently, we have not had to face a situation in which the Organization would not or could not act.

Self-Defense and Collective Defense

The Rio Treaty of 1947 was intended to be and is the principal document creating and governing a system of collective defense for all of the American states. It followed the lines agreed upon at Chapultepec in 1945; much of its language is identical with the NATO treaty negotiated about the same time.

The Chapultepec agreement had directly led to the inclusion, two months later, of the famous Article 51 in the Charter of the United Nations preserving "the inherent right of individual or collective self-defense," and of Article 52 which recognizes "regional arrangements or agencies for dealing with such matters relating to the maintenance of international peace and security as are appropriate for regional action."

Essentially the Rio Treaty was designed (a) to affirm the right of each state to defend itself against attack; (b) to establish the principle that an attack on any American state was an attack on all American states enabling them all to act at once; (c) to set up an obligation on all American states to defend any American state attacked, though no country could be required to use armed force without its consent. All countries can, however, be constrained by a two-thirds vote of the Organ of Consultation to put into effect sanctions short of armed force (breaking relations, cutting communications, and so forth).

These rights and obligations do not conflict with the principle of "nonintervention," which relates to measures not taken under the principle of individual or collective self-defense. The latter principle is necessarily supreme and overriding. No country has abandoned its right to its defense, or its right, in event of attack, to determine when, where, and how that defense shall be carried on. Since "attack" on any American state is stated in the Treaty of Rio to be attack on all American states, the right of defense by any American state exists when any other American state is attacked. An attack on Cuba, for example, would immediately give rise to the right of the United States to defend herself, as well as to defend Cuba. It would not, however, compel the United States to go to the defense of Cuba, unless the Organization of American States so voted. The United States (or any other American state) cannot be compelled under the Rio Treaty to use armed force in the defense of another country without its consent.

Recently it has become fashionable to maintain that the non-intervention clause of the Charter of Bogotá cancels the right of the United States to defend another American state against aggression, even in exercise of its own right of self-defense. At this point, Article 15 would become absurd—unless it had been intended to cancel most of the Treaty of Rio de Janeiro. This, of course, was not the case: Article 18 and Article 25 of the Charter of Bogotá specifically refer to and recognize "existing treaties" on the subject of self-defense, meaning, of course, the Treaty of Rio.

No more tenable is another interpretation sometimes put forward: that the right to defend any American state against aggression from outside, carried on through maintaining an internal revolution—or even the right of an American state (including the United States) to defend against such "internal aggression" in fact directed against itself—turns on receipt of a "request" from the government of the victim of such aggression. The argument does not stand up.

As between stranger states, one of which is attacked by another, a third state may not, without request, undertake defense of the state attacked. But, if the attack threatens the third state or is deemed to be an attack on the third state, it may defend itself, whether requested or not. Determination of the need for defense is based merely on its honest judgment. No country in the world, certainly not the United States or any country in Latin America, has yet agreed that it could not defend itself whenever it considered itself menaced without a "request" from someone else, still less without getting a vote authorizing its defense from some international group.

A pact of collective and reciprocal defense like that of Rio de Janeiro is, automatically, consent of the states involved that others may join in their defense, because all are considered equally attacked. Were the Soviet Union, for example, to seize Denmark overnight, the capacity of the United States and other NATO powers to act at once without waiting to see whether someone in Denmark would "request" defense would scarcely be questioned. For, in fact, these countries would not merely be defending Denmark; they would be defending each other and themselves as well. Judgment as to the necessity of that defense would belong to each one of them—not to any other group, or to the country whose government had thus been seized. Any other doctrine would paralyze the entire defensive apparatus so carefully thought out in the Treaty of Rio de Janeiro and the NATO treaty.

Section 1 of Article 3 of the Treaty of Rio de Janeiro provides:

> The High Contracting Parties agree that an armed attack by any State against an American State shall be considered as an attack against all the American States and, consequently, each one of the said Contracting Parties undertakes to assist in meeting the attack in the exercise of the inherent right of individual or collective self-defense recognized by Article 51 of the Charter of the United Nations.

It is to be noted that the right of individual or collective self-defense is exercisable at the determination of each individual state, or any group of them, or of any number of states who have joined a collective self-defense pact—as all American states joined in the Treaty of Rio.

Section 2 of Article 3 of the Treaty of Rio provides:

> On the request of the State or States directly attacked and until the decision of the Organ of Consultation of the Inter-American System, each one of the Contracting Parties may determine the immediate measures which it may individually take in fulfillment of the obligation contained in the preceding paragraph and in accordance with the principle of continental solidarity. . . .

This sets up a limitation on the obligation contained in the first paragraph of Article 3, by which all hands undertake to assist any country attacked. Article 20 of the Rio Treaty provides that no state shall be required under its provisions to use armed force in self-defense without its consent. Where collective action is asked, the request of the state attacked is needed. As an attack on any state is defined to be an attack on all American states, any state may invoke the Rio Treaty and demand a meeting of foreign ministers. Meanwhile, it can defend itself against the attack, alone or in collaboration with others, though the immediate military attack may be on some other American state.

The words "armed attack" were used advisedly. The Treaty of Rio, as noted, had been blocked out at the Chapultepec Conference. All of the parties had lived through a period in which the Nazi-Fascist powers had conducted armed attack chiefly by organizing and supporting internal insurrection without bothering to declare "war." Their recollections of Germany's organization of an internal coup in Austria prior to seizure and of the tearing to pieces of Czechoslovakia by creating an internal rebellion were still vivid. The attempts to do the same thing in Uruguay, in Bolivia, and in other situations were a matter of direct Latin American discussion and (as the writer, a member of the U.S. delegation at Chapultepec, can testify) were present in everyone's mind. The words "armed attack" were therefore used in the Treaty of Rio because the framers of the treaty, rightly, believed that a modern aggressor would not declare war and might not necessarily move troops or force under his own flag.

This was the interpretation placed on the Treaty of Rio de Janeiro at the time of its adoption. Though no hearings were held prior to the vote of ratification which passed the U.S. Senate unanimously on the report of the American delegation to that conference, its language was discussed a little later (April 27 to May 3, 1949) when the North Atlantic Treaty, with a similar clause, came up for ratification. A colloquy took place between Senator Fulbright of the Foreign Relations Committee and the Secretary of State, Dean Acheson. Acheson had made the point that the "inherent right of individual and collective self-defense" (the words are identical, both in the North Atlantic and the Rio treaties and in the U.N. Charter) was a complete, absolute right, not associated with regional arrangements. Then:

> *Senator Fulbright.* Under article 5 a question was prepared by the staff: Would an internal revolution, perhaps aided and abetted by an outside state, in which armed force was being used in an attempt to drive the recognized government from power be deemed an "armed attack" within the meaning of article 5?
>
> That is a little different from the last question, in that I assume an ordinary election which the Communists won. This is in the nature of a coup. Would that come within the definition of an armed attack? . . .
>
> *Secretary Acheson.* I think it would be an armed attack.
>
> *Senator Fulbright.* It would be?
>
> *Secretary Acheson.* It would seem to me that it would, yes.
>
> *Senator Fulbright.* Would you say that each country, or this country, would decide for itself whether or not that is an armed attack within the meaning of article 5, or would that be a function of the Council?
>
> *Secretary Acheson.* No. Each country would have to decide for itself.

Lest there be doubt that the same interpretation prevailed with respect to the Rio Treaty as with respect to the North Atlantic Treaty, the testimony made clear that the precedent for the North

Atlantic Treaty was found in the Rio pact. Secretary Acheson indeed testified that treaties did not "create the right of individual or collective self-defense. That is inherent in all nations. . . . These arrangements that I have referred to, the Rio Treaty, the Brussels Treaty, and this treaty [the North Atlantic Treaty] are arrangements entered into as an exercise of the inherent right of individual and collective self-defense," and the treaties are not limitative.[6]

Both in the preliminary negotiations from Chapultepec on and when the Rio Treaty was ratified, a "coup" aided and abetted from outside and involving the use of armed force was considered an "armed attack" giving rise to the right of both individual and collective self-defense. Action for that purpose is not "intervention" under Article 15 of the Bogotá Charter.

Exposition is here made at length because, at present as in the decade of the Nazi aggressions, the strategy of the aggressor is simple. As in Cuba, he conceals his armed operations by introducing them as subversive forces within the victim country, and he screamingly maintains that any defense against such operations is a violation of peace, and of international law, and is "intervention." The Soviet Union and Communist China are doing exactly this in their military encroachments on Laos and Viet-Nam; the Soviet Union, both directly and through Castro, is invoking the same argument now in connection with Cuba.

[6] *North Atlantic Treaty*, Hearings before the Senate Committee on Foreign Relations, 81st Cong., 1st sess., April 27-May 3, 1949, Pt. 1 (Washington: GPO, 1949), pp. 15, 31, 58-59, 243 and *passim*.

Chapter VI

The Inter-American
System in Crisis

The inter-American system is in crisis. Its existence, as well
as its capacity, is at stake. This is not the result of the Punta del
Este Conference of 1962; that conference merely recognized the
crisis and laid outlines of struggle toward its solution. The problem itself is the problem of confronting the cold war.

Determination to seek control of the Western Hemisphere was
taken by the two principal Communist powers some years ago.
Propaganda, infiltration, and organization have been quietly going forward. Opening of the Latin American "front" has been
confirmed by the pronouncements of both Soviet and Chinese
leaders in 1959 and 1960. Public opinion in the United States
has not even yet appreciated the seriousness of that decision.
Our own country has appeared to consider that cold wars with
their ultimate phase of armed action occur only in Southeast
Asia, in the Near East, or perhaps in Africa. Latin American
thinking has followed somewhat the same line. In any case, in
Latin America it is always difficult to distinguish between indigenous social revolutionary activity and disorder induced from
overseas in the interest of Communist conquest. In 1961, however, the overseas intrusion became overt. Capacity to meet it will
determine the fate of the inter-American system on whose existence the present policy of the United States is based.

* * *

The issue, of course, was precipitated by affairs in Cuba. The
revolution led by Fidel Castro against the dictatorship of Ful-
gencio Batista was in its initial phase primarily if not purely a
Cuban revolution. In 1958 Castro's forces were receiving help

from outside, chiefly from Mexico; but this was clandestine, and it came from non-Communist groups interested in setting up a democratic regime in and for Cuba. On December 2, 1961, Fidel Castro confessed in a public speech that he had all along intended to make his revolution a Marxist-Leninist revolution, on the side of "socialism" and the great Soviet Union and against "imperialism." He also boasted that he had lied about this for the purpose of deceiving his Cuban supporters, including his own guerrillas. Arrived in power on January 1, 1959, with the indispensable help of thousands of non-Communist Cubans, he promptly proceeded with the work of betraying the native Cuban revolution into overseas Communist hands.

As early as March 1959, some of his colleagues were already convinced that this was his plan and took refuge outside Cuba, to be followed by many others. Castro, meanwhile, was still asserting (falsely as he now states) first, that he was not a Communist or allied to outside powers, and, second, that it was an outrageous act of "provocative aggression" for anyone to accuse him of it. By 1960, only the most gullible could continue to believe that Castro had not replaced the first, announced democratic revolution by a Communist one, or fail to realize that he was receiving money, arms, military personnel, and assurance of aid from the extra-continental Communist powers and was turning Cuba into a satellite of their imperial system.

Officially at least, most other Latin American governments did not take this view. They insisted that the case had yet to be proved; or that they did not know, or otherwise. At all events, most of the governments south of the Panama Canal officially treated the Cuban situation as merely another indigenous Latin American revolution. Whether any of them really believed this interpretation or merely adopted it for diplomatic purposes is a matter of conjecture. Fidel Castro's own boastful account, in December 1961, of his Communist coup left no possibility for further doubt.

By that time several Latin American governments were themselves concerned. Peru had forced the issue by moving in the Council of the O.A.S. to convoke a meeting of the foreign ministers of the American states to take up the conduct of the Cuban government, by then in alignment with the Sino-Soviet bloc, as an instance of aggression under the Rio Treaty; meanwhile, the Council was to appoint a committee to investigate in Cuba the violations of inter-American agreements charged by Peru in its complaint. This move collided with a more cautious move of the government of Colombia. That government had planned to propose a similar meeting, but it was designed to lay a foundation for sanctions against Cuba by first clarifying the vexed interrelationship of the problems of "intervention" and defense, and by affording Cuba opportunity, by changing her ways, to return to the inter-American system if she desired. The O.A.S. Council, overcoming a delaying campaign, finally agreed to vote on December 4. Its further avoidance of the issue was made impossible by vigorous action of the six Central American states, which rightly estimated their own safety was in peril. Just prior to the vote came Castro's famous speech—"I am a Marxist-Leninist, and I will be [one] to the last day of my life."—an act of calculated defiance.

By December 4, there was thus no longer a possibility of evading the issue. The O.A.S. Council voted on a Colombian resolution requesting a conference to serve as Organ of Consultation in accordance with the Treaty of Rio, "to consider the threats to the peace and to the political independence of the American states that might arise from the intervention of extra-continental powers directed toward breaking American solidarity."[1] It was carried by a bare majority. Two countries, Cuba and Mexico, voted "No." Bolivia, Chile, Brazil, Argentina and Ecuador abstained, nominally on technical grounds. What this came to was, of course, a split in the O.A.S., joined in by the three most populous Latin American countries. Whatever their official explanations, it was clear that the penetration of the hemisphere by the extra-continental Communist powers was not an issue they wished to face.

It was certain that neither Mexico nor Brazil then intended that the meeting, when held, would take serious action, and only a possibility that Argentina would favor such action. The smaller countries, whose independent life depends on that system implemented by the force of the United States, urgently

[1] Pan American Union, *Eighth Meeting of Consultation of Ministers of Foreign Affairs, Final Act* (Washington: Author, 1962), pp. 1-2.

desired maintenance of the inter-American system—but they could no longer count on it.

Perhaps the most revealing comment during the whole affair was made by the Mexican representative on the O.A.S. Council in November 1961. In the debate upon the resolution offered by Colombia, proposing a meeting of foreign ministers to discuss and to define attacks and aggressions, and on the stronger Peruvian proposal, he came right out with it, saying that Mexico was not willing to go along. In any case, he said, the Organization of American States was not strong enough to sustain the burden of decisions of this nature. Therefore, it should avoid such issues.

Unhappily, issues of this kind do not disappear because a regional organization does not meet them. When matters as vital as defense are involved, failure of an international body to deal with them merely means that each individual state must fend for itself, in agreement with such adherents as it can find, or acting alone in case of necessity. The precise result would be to leave the various American republics to deal separately with their own defense in the international conflict we call (euphemistically) the cold war, according to their respective national capacities and interests. Included among the nations thus pushed back to their own resources would be, of course, the United States. Faced with a choice between adjourning the conference, as division appeared, and meeting the problem, the United States determined to push ahead though few in the American delegation indulged illusions about the results.

The chief opposing states—Mexico, Brazil, Argentina, Bolivia, Chile and Ecuador—were not prepared to vote for sanctions against Cuba. Perhaps they could not prevent a two-thirds vote requiring all members to impose such sanctions, but sanctions were not likely to be very effective if those countries opposed. But there was a higher measure of agreement for a nonoperative resolution declaring that Cuba, dominated by an overseas Communist system, was a regime incapable of working within the inter-American system. And it appeared possible to exclude the Communist government of Cuba from the Organization of American States.

In that situation, the Punta del Este Conference met on January 22, 1962. The American delegation, wisely in the writer's opinion, decided not to ask for full sanctions, but also wisely determined not to be satisfied with mere words of a nonoperative resolution of censure. It therefore sought a resolution excluding the current Cuban regime from the councils of the Organization of American States. Exploratory attempts to work out language which would induce a favorable vote by Argentina, Brazil, Chile, and Mexico failed. Again rightly, in the writer's opinion, the United States determined to stand its ground in open conference. Had it not done so, the Central American states might well have left.

The Punta del Este Conference took three major decisions:

First, it adopted without a negative vote, except Cuba's (though Ecuador abstained), a resolution declaring the Communist regime in Cuba "incompatible" with its membership in the inter-American system: a clear-cut victory on a point of principle.

Second, it adopted a resolution, by a vote of fourteen to six, directing the Council of the O.A.S. to exclude the Cuban regime from further participation in inter-American meetings. The six abstainers were the six original objectors: Mexico, Brazil, Argentina, Chile, Bolivia and Ecuador. It is interesting that they abstained; neither legal scruples nor political considerations proved strong enough to bring them to vote against the resolution. Privately their delegates explained that they agreed with the United States in principle but differed as to the means of restoring hemispheric unity. Some at least thought that negotiation with Cuba would achieve some result.

Third, it agreed that the American states should suspend immediately all trade with Cuba in arms and implements of war.[2]

A number of other measures were taken, including setting up a "watchdog" committee designed, among other things, to provide information on cold war efforts. It was also evident that many Latin American delegates at Punta del Este personally

2 Same, pp. 12-16.

agreed with the position of the United States, although prevented from voting in accordance with their convictions by instructions of their governments. The positive result was a clear-cut expression of opposition to overseas Communist imperialism, joined in by nineteen countries. The division of opinion turned on how, and how far, that opposition should be made concrete. All in all, this was a victory for the United States position.

The effect of the Punta del Este Conference was to give the inter-American system a respectable fighting chance to establish itself. Its "incompatibility" resolution stated a platform for hemispheric defense. Its exclusion of the Castro regime eliminated a continuing avenue of sabotage; lack of unanimity there made no difference in the result: the Cuban regime remains well and duly excluded. Approval of arms control measures made possible arrangements for defense against the now familiar Communist tactics of force.

On the positive side, there is the agreement on the program for the Alliance for Progress, adopted at the earlier Punta del Este Conference of 1961.

This combination forms a nucleus around which the constructive forces in all of the countries of the hemisphere can gather. How rapidly they began to do so can be judged by immediate pressures compelling President Frondizi of Argentina to break relations with Castro. These came within weeks after Punta del Este had ended. There has also been a mounting political movement in Brazil generally oriented toward maintaining her classic friendship with the United States, although Brazil's course remains uncertain. Punta del Este was not the end of anything, nor the resolution of anything. Nor could it have been. But it was the effective beginning of a campaign to re-create hemispheric solidarity and to restore the inter-American system. On its outcome depends the system's fate.

As Mexico pointed out prior to Punta del Este, the question remains whether the Organization of American States can sustain the burden forced by the decision of the Communist powers to challenge freedom in this hemisphere. Of that challenge there is now no doubt. This was the purpose of Castro's declaration in Havana on February 5, calling for continental civil war, and of the prearranged support given this call by the Soviet Union, speaking through Nikita Khrushchev.

Criticism has been expressed because the United States accepted the Punta del Este Conference in the first place, division among the Latin American states being likely, and because it went through with a policy which necessarily put that division of opinion on record. This criticism is not justified. For one thing, the six Central American states were rapidly becoming desperate. If the inter-American system had reached a stage where it could not or would not function to protect them, they were prepared to walk out and try to protect themselves in some other way. Acceptance of anything less than the Punta del Este resolution excluding the Cuban Communist regime would probably have forced this result, and Peru might have joined them. The six Central American states with Peru and Colombia had demanded the meeting under a plain treaty right. Refusal to go forward with the Punta del Este meeting might of itself have precipitated dissolution of the inter-American system. Division of opinion notoriously existed; holding or not holding the conference would not change that fact; better indeed to recognize the situation and get to work on it. Given the circumstances, the United States and the inter-American system with it came out as well as the political facts permitted. Far better, in fact, than if the O.A.S. had declared bankruptcy by being unable to meet, or had demonstrated its impotence by agreeing only on a meaningless formula of words.

A crucial fact was that several of the six governments abstaining from voting on the resolution excluding the Castro regime from the inter-American councils did so not because of inherent disagreement, but because their internal situation was such that their governments felt they could not act. In Brazil, the government headed by President João Goulart and Premier Tancredo Neves had been precipitately put together as a result of former President Quadros' ill-timed resignation. What it represents in terms of Brazilian opinion is unclear—as much so in Brasilia as at Punta del Este. A recent revolution in Ecuador had put its Vice-President Arosemena into the presidency amid a tangle of unresolved forces seeking dominance, a government without a mandate. Internal politics in Chile were so closely balanced that a strong stand by President Alessandri might shift the political balance in favor of anti-American groups which were politically almost as strong as he, as the 1958 elections and subsequent tests had shown. In Argentina, President Arturo Frondizi was maneuvering for position, doubtful whether he could keep the Peronista forces from breaking into disorderly opposition.

In most cases it is probable the "soft six" governments at Punta del Este abstained from the resolution directing the expulsion of Cuba less from conviction than from uncertainty as to their own political safety. In the case of Brazil, it is a fair probability that a majority of the population would support the position of the United States. (In 1941, the then Brazilian dictator, Getulio Vargas, hesitated nearly two years before popular opinion persuaded him to join the anti-Nazi alliance.) In Argentina, it is certain that powerful elements, including the army and navy, were in agreement with the United States.

Effectively, Punta del Este settled that a campaign to re-create the hemispheric system around the Alliance for Progress would be waged. As always, a positive policy commands respect.

An unhappy commentary on United States press coverage of Latin American affairs must be noted. During the Punta del Este Conference, and in retaliation for its being held, the overseas Communist apparatus called for and endeavored to bring off revolutions in Guatemala, in Venezuela, and in Nicaragua. Probably because the all-too-few American journalists on the Latin American scene were covering the Punta del Este Conference, this fact went almost unnoticed in the American press. Unnoticed, too, was the more significant fact that in every case the attempt proved abortive. In Guatemala the plot (which included assassination and guerrilla operations) was discovered and smashed though at date of writing (February 1962) a few guerrillas are still in the field. In Venezuela there were crackles of Communist revolt in a number of places, and twenty or thirty casualties were suffered in stifling them. The call to arms in Nicaragua got nowhere. The Dominican Republic, reaching a balance after the overthrow of the Trujillo regime, appeared to have the situation well in hand. The Communist countercampaign against

Punta del Este thus failed, though it will surely be renewed. Yet, though there was relative success at Punta del Este, it was clearly not decisive. In the face of a clear state of facts, the largest Latin American states did not wish or did not feel able to support measures comparable to the seriousness of the thrust, and their statesmen took refuge in evasions, exaggerated legalisms, and meaningless formulae. These were essentially incapable of being harmonized with the plain intent of the Rio Treaty and the Charter of Bogotá.

The treaties are there. On paper, a consensus of Western Hemisphere will has been reached, reduced to the language of these treaties, signed, sealed, delivered, and ratified. Probably all the countries involved, including those most vocal now in refusing to make the system effective, would claim that all of the obligations in these treaties they consider in their favor were still binding. Obviously all these obligations are part of a complete package, and the binding force of one part, if the other part of the package were relegated to meaningless nullity, would come into question. Failure of the treaties and with them of the inter-American system might well convert Latin America into a vast Balkan peninsula. The system has yet to demonstrate its capacity to prevent that result.

These are unpleasant observations. In fairness to the hesitant governments it should be observed that twenty-three years ago there was like hesitation by the United States, by Great Britain, and by most of Europe in confronting a similar issue tendered by Adolf Hitler. For that matter, American politicians more than a century ago fobbed off, as long as they could, the dangerous issue of slavery, nullification and the Kansas-Nebraska guerrilla warfare in the decade prior to the American Civil War. We must therefore understand and may absolve the Latin American politicians now involved in equivocal positions. But we cannot on that account avoid asking how far the Organization of American States will be effective, and what has to be done.

The rationale both of the Treaty of Rio and of the O.A.S. was to maintain regional peace *and* to protect the American hemisphere from overseas interference. To ignore this motivation is to ignore the principal reason for inter-American system.

The second basis of the system is no less important than the first, and no less involved in the current problem. The intent of all parties, the initiative coming from Colombia, was to guarantee the frontiers of every American state as among themselves —as well as against extra-continental powers. In part this may perhaps have been directed against the United States, although few serious Latin American statesmen then feared, or now fear, that the United States would seize territory. They were not quite so sure about each other. When the Treaty of Rio de Janeiro and the Charter of Bogotá were signed, however, every boundary question had been settled, save only a claim by Nicaragua for a small strip of land on the boundary of Honduras. As long as hemispheric affairs are dealt with by the states of the hemisphere itself, regional peace-keeping is comparatively simple. But if a claimant for territory, defying the mutual guarantee of frontiers, chooses to call in an extra-continental power, the difficulty of peace-keeping can be immensely increased. Once the hemispheric line is broken, any kind of complication may arise—as they have historically arisen in that breeding ground of war, the Balkan peninsula. Castro has now broken it. Others may try to follow his example; thus, some Ecuadoran politicians have recently flirted with the idea of invoking Communist help in Ecuador's boundary dispute with Peru, which was settled twenty years ago but has recently broken out anew.

An international body afraid to meet an issue has an immense armory of diplomatic procedures and weapons enabling it to avoid action. Whatever the moves, they are all veiled ways of saying that the body either cannot, is afraid to, or does not wish to, take action. The simplest maneuver is to ask for elaborate fact-finding procedures, though the facts are clear—as a litigant in a law suit will use the legal procedure of demanding sworn proof of his signature to delay meeting his obligation to pay a note. Another is to refer the matter to an obviously impotent committee to consider legality or procedure. When such measures mean no action while the use of force is taking place, they are equivalent to a resolution to consider locking the barn door after it is clear that the horse is stolen and the thieves are somewhere else—but taking care to do nothing while the thieves might be put under restraint.

The Organization of American States has no monopoly on this kind of evasion. The old League of Nations resorted to it in Mussolini's time. The United Nations also can do pretty well at it, as the reaction to the Soviet explosion of atomic bombs, or to the Indian occupation of Portuguese territories, recently showed. But when extra-continental interference in the hemisphere is involved, avoidance of the issue is equivalent to denial by the O.A.S. of the law of its being. The fact, for instance, that a guerrilla army, organized, planned, and financed from outside the hemisphere, chooses to fly a local flag does not change the fact of extra-continental aggression.

It has been the policy of the government of the United States to endeavor to use, strengthen, and maintain the Organization of American States. Can it continue to do so?

A substantial measure of unity exists. Condemnation of the Communist solution is almost unanimous. All the Latin American countries except Cuba have affirmed a common economic policy and solidarity in their search for stated economic and social objectives at the meeting of the Inter-American Economic and Social Council at Punta del Este in August 1961. The catalyzing core of this affirmation was the offer of assistance by the United States contemplated in the program known as the Alliance for Progress, to which the Council will provide continuing coordination and staff work although the real activities will be in the hands of the Inter-American Development Bank and the U.S. agencies such as AID and the Export-Import Bank.

Affirmation of support for the Alliance for Progress contemplates the continuing existence of the inter-American system. But the program outlined can hardly exist, nor can it have much hope of effective result if, simultaneously, the signatory governments fall victims to political movements or armed revolts aimed primarily at making them hostile to the United States, or at undermining the stability and paralyzing the effectiveness of the governments and economic systems through which the resources of the Alliance for Progress must be administered. Bitter denunciation of that plan by Castro's Cuba corresponds to the bitter denunciation of the Marshall Plan in 1947 by the Soviet Union at the conference which met in Paris to set up the European organization that later so effectively administered the Marshall Plan assistance. Communist-dominated governments do not cooperate in plans of this kind now any more than in 1947. It is likewise impossible to expect Communist-dominated parties of opposition in Latin American countries not to oppose effective organization of economic programs administered by the governments they aim to overthrow. Yet the largest Latin American governments still waver. With the conclusion of the Punta del Este Conference of January 1962, the issue is joined, but the outcome is not yet determined.

Lest the prospect seem too bleak, it must be remembered that in the decade of the thirties a similar situation was successfully faced. Then, the inter-American system meant little more than periodic conferences held by the Pan American Union, and a loose system of "consultation" worked out by President Roosevelt and the Latin American states at the Conference of Buenos Aires in 1936. Consultation meant only an obligation of all parties to discuss common problems, with no obligation whatever to reach agreement. In that situation, the Nazi-Fascist powers endeavored to establish their domination over various parts of the hemisphere. When the Second World War broke out, there was substantial division of opinion among the American group of nations. Only eight countries declared war on Germany after Pearl Harbor. These were all Caribbean countries, from Panama north, and did not include Mexico. There was also intense political activity within each one of the republics. Nazi or Fascist parties were organized in all, with the avowed end of influencing the governments to side with the Axis powers against Great Britain and France and, after Pearl Harbor, against the United States.

Then, as now, many Latin American countries, including the largest (Mexico, Brazil, Chile and Argentina) hesitated and talked "neutrality." Later they asked help from the United States. In the ensuing three years, all eventually joined the hemispheric bloc although Argentina, despite her declaration of war on Germany, really maintained a position of overt neutrality weighted on the German side. If we assume that the inter-American system, as represented by the O.A.S. under the Treaty of Rio de Janeiro and the Charter of Bogotá, cannot act, the position of the United States is not very different from that it held against the attacking Nazi powers from 1939 through World War II. Any difference lies in the fact that the potential of Communist revolutions and guerrilla wars in the Latin American republics probably is substantially greater than was the Nazi potential in 1938. Three years of steady, clear-sighted, and firm diplomacy directed by Secretary Cordell Hull eventually brought most of the hemisphere into a common policy of opposing the would-be world dominators of the time. Today much of the task has to be done again. It is not easy. But it is by no means impossible.

No country in the Western Hemisphere, so far as the writer is aware, has yet visualized or has faced the implications of a possible breakdown of the inter-American system. The consequences could be as bloody as they would be far-reaching. The government of Colombia, until recently headed by President Alberto Lleras Camargo, probably has thought the problem through more deeply than any other, including our own, perhaps a natural reflection of the fact that the original conception resulting in the Treaty of Rio de Janeiro came from a great Colombian—the idea was proposed by President Eduardo Santos to and promptly adopted by President Franklin Roosevelt.

The small countries of Central America are already reacting. Militarily weak, they know their peaceful existence depends on protection in case of need by an inter-American system backed if necessary by the force it can muster; or, failing effective inter-American action, on protection directly by the United States. With failure of the system, Central America could be torn to pieces. Major repercussions would also be felt on the west coast of South America—perhaps are already in sight. Ecuador's government is equivocal. The dispute between Ecuador and Peru over the Amazon provinces could under Communist agitation flare into direct hostilities—as indeed it did in 1941. Communist intrigue already enters into the discussions. In the absence of effective peace-keeping capacity in the inter-American system, the results might be tragic. To these add the complications of existing internal movements in several countries, elements of which receive overseas Communist arms, money and "expenses" via Cuba—and one can visualize the possibility of a South American edition of the terrible Spanish civil war.

The greatest gift of the inter-American system, even in its early and formative phases, was to diminish the possibility of this kind of struggle. Or, when struggle did break out, to limit it. That was done in the case of the Chaco War between Bolivia and Paraguay in the decade of the thirties.

American observers find it difficult to claim objectivity. Regarding the situation with as much detachment as they can, they wonder in all seriousness whether the policy of some Latin American political leaders does not border on dangerous absurdity (as, of course, U.S. policy did in not facing up promptly to the implications of Nazism in Europe). When they abandon the relative security of the inter-American system, they enter a trackless, bloody jungle of world politics. Militarily, no Latin American state is able to cope with any serious threat from outside. Economically, their situation is vulnerable. A great European Common Market has been born. The members of that Common Market consider that it should have preferential relations with their now liberated colonies in Africa. This means that markets formerly supplied largely by Latin America will increasingly be reserved to the new countries, notably African, issuing from the nineteenth-century colonial system. These countries as it happens produce precisely the commodities which Latin American nations have had to export and must at present continue to sell to satisfy their import needs. Increasingly hindered from selling in the European Common Market, they are increasingly dependent on markets in the United States. The propensity of some Latin American politicians toward nullifying the inter-American system, or picking quarrels with the United States, could hardly accord less with current Latin American economic as well as military reality.

Some Latin Americans will reply that they are in process of constructing, and will rely on, their own common market. This is desirable; and the Latin American movement in that direction is deserving of help. It is receiving only lukewarm support from Brazil, whose government hopes to join the European Common

Market though she has not been invited. But the European Common Market came into existence to coordinate and broaden the activities of industry whose plants and organizations were already constructed. It contemplates a high degree of political cooperation. The Latin American common market is coming into existence literally for the purpose of building industries now largely nonexistent. A substantial period of time must elapse before the structure can reach a measure of collective self-sufficiency liberating these countries from the necessity of imports from or of markets in either Europe or the United States, and of creating political cooperation suggesting permanence.

Latin American countries may also turn to the Communist powers. Few who are familiar with the ferocious exploitation of underdeveloped countries which have dealt with the barter markets of the Communist bloc would maintain seriously that exchange between Latin America and the Communist countries could replace the exchange Latin American countries now have with the United States, or that even a self-contained Latin American common market would fare at all well in that kind of arrangement. Soviet exploitation was a major reason why Yugoslavia broke with Moscow; Guinea and other African countries that welcomed Russia's aid later found themselves in open conflict with her; Red China is already in default on her economic commitments.

The government of the United States, of course, has to cope with the public opinion in the United States. That opinion is beginning to be formed by a growing, though still incomplete, body of information as to what Latin Americans say and do in their own countries. It reads, or hears on television, pro-Communist or anti-Yankee speeches. It recognizes the right of any Latin American from Mexico to Argentina to be anti-Yankee if he wishes. But anti-Yankee movements south of the border do not predispose American citizens to write their Congressmen urging huge appropriations for the Alliance for Progress, or supporting quota or price stabilization arrangements designed to favor Latin American sellers at the expense of the American consumer.

* * *

The year 1962, therefore, is witnessing a fateful test of the inter-American system and of the classic unity prescribed for the hemisphere by Simón Bolívar and promptly supported by Brazil nearly a century and a half ago. The system is plowing through heavy seas. Yet its cracks are not irreparable. The policy of the United States in seeking that the issues be faced rather than avoided seems unassailable. One remembers that the League of Nations, when it failed to confront the problem of Mussolini's attack on Ethiopia in 1936, signed its own death warrant. A second world war was needed to make possible a new attempt.

Chapter VII

Prospects for the Western Hemisphere

1. THE NEARBY SCENE

Parallel has already been drawn between the situation prevailing in Europe when organization of the Marshall Plan took place in the teeth of organized Communist violence, and that prevailing today in Latin America as the Alliance for Progress gets under way. Now, as then, companion problems of construction and defense must be simultaneously solved.

This is not well understood in the United States. One line of opinion, vigorously urged in certain journals and by certain commentators, insists that the task of the United States is not directly to oppose Communist imperialism but to remove the conditions —poverty, ignorance, disorganization—which breed communism and create the conditions which encourage progress and democracy. Basically this idea is sound, but it lends itself to escapist thinking, all too attractive in a very naughty world. The United States did not, does not, probably should not "create" the conditions in the several Latin American countries; they alone can do that. She could not do so by herself unless she were prepared to conquer and administer an empire—a method wholly foreign to her inclination, her experience, and to the modern world. One may discard as unworthy of serious attention insistence by left-wing American intellectuals that mere extension of trade and financial relations is automatically "imperialist."

Elimination of conditions that breed communism will require at best a substantial number of years. In Puerto Rico, where this result has been achieved, serious reorganization began during the governorship of Rexford Guy Tugwell and got under way effectively under that of Governor Luis Muñoz Marín and his administration of the reconstituted Estado Libre Associado. Substantial and tangible effects under the planned economy of the island only became visible some years after the original conception. Now, ten years after the institution of the Estado Libre, the results are brilliant. But no one familiar either with the Communist empires or the Latin American scene has any illusion that either the Soviet Union or the Chinese empire will adjourn the cold war in Latin America to permit unimpeded advance of the work of the Alliance for Progress.

Well-being is pleasanter to think about than defense. But the cold war has been declared. Overseas as well as hemispheric operations are now in full blast, including planning, preparing, mounting, and in some areas directing, active guerrilla warfare. These operations are designed to conquer and to keep. There is thus no alternative to providing and maintaining defense, even as the Alliance for Progress is being organized and goes forward. At least since the year 1956, cadres of Latin Americans have been trained in Communist China. Other cadres were indoctrinated and trained for operation at least as early as 1949. Preparations for a major offensive in Latin America are, if anything, more complete in 1962 than were Soviet preparations for the capture of Western Europe in 1947.

The Communist campaign may run into difficulties, as mounting rivalry between Moscow and Peiping reaches the stage of open hostility. A break or open conflict between the two titans of the Marxist-Leninist area might affect the Latin American picture, where Chinese and Soviet Russian propaganda and their recruiting machines are already in covert but crackling opposition. But it does not follow that such conflict would put an end to the Communist struggle to overthrow all regimes save their own. The possibility should not change U.S. plans, either for hemispheric defense or for the Alliance for Progress, or those of the other states, committed to both.

Organization and Resources for Action

Surveying the scene, the first glance ought to be at the United States and her own organization.

The fact is that the United States, at the moment, does not have adequate organization to deal rapidly and effectively with the categories of problems which the Alliance for Progress must solve. She is on the way to forging one, but the work has far to go.

The United States has substantial resources of the trained men that are needed. Herein her position is more advantageous than when the Good Neighbor policy was outlined in 1933. A good many universities now maintain departments or institutes of Latin American affairs. A growing volume of analytical literature, basic and current, is now readily available. A particularly large reservoir of effective men exists in Puerto Rico, graduates of Governor Muñoz Marín's intensive school of political and social reconstruction. American business has developed a substantial number of young men trained in particular techniques and capable of understanding Latin American points of view on most questions. It should therefore be possible to recruit the personnel needed to work with the Latin American personnel of the Alliance for Progress' local and hemisphere-wide mechanisms as they develop.

Available personnel, of course, does not mean adequacy of existing organization. Washington bureaucracy, like all bureaucracy, moves ponderously. (Khrushchev once endeavored to persuade Nehru that he had best shift sides in the cold war specifically because the U.S. government in its clumsiness could not act at all in many crucial situations, and in most others could not act in time.) Yet, when it must, it can pull itself together. In the spring of 1961, when Bolivia was on the eve both of revolution and of economic dissolution, a task force was organized, was sent to La Paz, developed a plan and put it into execution in the space of about four weeks. But that was done on the personal order of President Kennedy, against a muted obbligato of protest from the lesser Department of State bureaucracy, their objection being that "orderly" administrative processes were interrupted. In point of fact, the operation probably saved Bolivia from civil war. Like political machines in the United States, many bureaucracies would rather lose a campaign than lose control of the organization.

Four categories of trained men, capable of constituting teams for specific pieces of work, will be needed.

1. *Economic and social.* Of first importance are those who will work on problems of economic planning, including banking, currency, taxation, budget making, business financing in private sector operations, grant and public loan financing in social sector operations. Their principal foci in Washington will be the Inter-American Development Bank, the AID regional organization for Latin America now headed by a brilliant Puerto Rican, Teodoro Moscoso, who carried out the Puerto Rican "Operation Bootstrap," the Treasury, and the Export-Import Bank under the very able leadership of Harold Linder.

These men will be working with opposite numbers in the country or countries whose problems are being tackled. They will influence the financial decisions and operations of the Alliance for Progress. But it must be recognized that their greatest contribution must be intellectual.

The next eight or nine years of the Alliance for Progress should see the allocation of perhaps twenty billion *in toto* of American resource, public and private. But outside capital, even on so large a scale, cannot guarantee success. The United States for the year 1962 will expend at home about $29 billion of capital in its private sector alone. Obviously the success of the Alliance for Progress policy must depend mainly on mobilizing, increasing, and allocating the capital resources formed and to be formed by the Latin American countries themselves. This can be done. But it is a political, intellectual, and economic task of a high order.

2. *Educational.* A substantial body of experts, backed by adequate resources to develop teacher training and to make available teaching materials, is needed for educational organization and progress in Latin America. It is the writer's belief that there exists a considerable number (though not enough) of such people in the United States capable of working with their Latin American colleagues. Many of them, perhaps, have as much to learn as to teach when it comes to direct application. It is highly un-

likely that Latin America will, and no valid reason why she should, abandon her European-oriented intellectual habits and methods for those advocated by many teachers' colleges in the United States. American educators will find school systems and educational campaigns in countries like Venezuela and Mexico that command high respect. They will discover all manner of facets of the educational problem. They will emerge with tremendous respect for the abilities and devotion of their Latin American colleagues, which can only enhance the value of the advice and service they themselves can give.

3. *Organization of military cooperation.* In some ways, the military sector of U.S. policy is already the most highly developed, and most cooperatively organized. So-called "military assistance programs" between the United States and most of the Latin American countries have been going forward already for a good many years. The contacts have been fruitful. It has been observed elsewhere in these pages that Latin American armies do not get their just due from American opinion. This is because, like armies everywhere, they cannot govern and usually make a mess of it when they try. Most men in them are as patriotic and as dedicated to forwarding the welfare of their own country as any group of citizens. Most regard themselves, and in fact have acted, as guardians of constitutional civil government since 1950— in the case of Brazil, since 1945. In the main, the young officers represent the growing Latin American middle class.

These armies, like our own, must now meet the nasty problem of political guerrilla warfare supported from overseas. This means they must not only fight guerrillas but must help to produce the political atmosphere essential to success in that fight, as the late President Magsaysay did in the Philippine republic a few years ago. Most Latin American armies know this better than we; they have been reckoning with the possibility, or dealing with the fact, of guerrilla action for a long time. U.S. military cooperation will have to be increasingly cast in these terms.

Of direct and immediate importance will be expanded cooperation in arms traffic control designed to interrupt the steady trickle of Soviet guns, munitions, and terrorist weapons from

Cuba primarily to the Latin American countries bordering the Caribbean littoral and to Ecuador. This will be a complex job. Joint sea patrols can stop ships and take off contraband in the territorial waters of any of the cooperating countries. Joint air patrols can locate the clandestine fields where the "black" planes by night land secret shipments of arms and munitions. Joint intelligence operations can give information. Such measures were taken and were effective in World War II, to prevent the clandestine operations of Nazi Germany. So also were the measures of economic warfare taken in conjunction with them to cut down the resources available within the hemisphere to the enemy for financing his propaganda and other operations. Today, of course, technical developments require a higher degree of mutual confidence, but the problems are similar and can be dealt with if that confidence exists.

4. *Propaganda.* Not within the Alliance for Progress, but strictly within control of the United States, there must and should be organization for direct political propaganda. Latin Americans expect this. Many are surprised and bewildered because it has not come into existence. This is not to replace or substitute for the American "information" program. That stands on its own feet. Within the limits of its resources, it has done a very respectable job. But it does not offer a direct means of advocacy which pulls no punches and is not afraid of its U.S. sponsorship. This sponsorship is important precisely because a propaganda agency does plead the U.S. cause. It may include frank ownership of certain Latin American newspapers. Communist-owned newspapers exist; and everyone knows them, their sponsorship, their reason for existence. It has been assumed in some quarters that direct American ownership of anything automatically exposes it to attack. That is true, but not important: everything American is, or will shortly be, under attack by the propaganda systems of the overseas Communist empires.

We have come, I think, to the end of a road. At Punta del Este the issue was joined, and war promptly declared by Havana in Castro's speech of February 4, 1962. The United States at once became a central element in the group attempting to maintain the integrity of the American system. She, with like-minded governments, parties, and individuals, is expected, indeed urged, to state her case. Obviously, her case will also be the case for the Alliance for Progress.

The Political Struggle

Long before the organization has shaken down, the first phase of the political campaign extending throughout all Latin America will have taken place. It has begun already; probably will be well advanced by the time these pages reach print. In the existing state of U.S. press coverage, American public opinion will have only fragmentary knowledge of its progress. At this stage, what goes on in labor unions, in the various political parties, in student organizations, in the press, in military clubs, on the streets, will have greater importance than the formal diplomatic attitudes of governments and palace political news. The ultimate results of these superficially minor events will, to be sure, have their effect on the positions and attitudes of these governments, which will reflect the decisions of dominant forces: intellectual, popular, military, or all three.

We know already the general lines of the campaign, and that, despite differences in various areas, the general overseas Communist strategy will be much the same everywhere. As in the decade of the thirties, attempts will be made to eliminate the "middle ground"—liberal democracy as the United States knows it. On that point extreme right, or Fascist elements, already agree with the extreme left, or Communist elements, each claiming to be the "wave of the future." Where tactically advantageous, the two extremes will ally with each other, though this will not prevent each wing from planning to destroy its ally if and when they are jointly successful. This is what occurred in Europe as the Nazi government converged on the Hitler-Stalin pact in 1939, and again at the end of World War II. The tactic reappeared after the Marshall Plan was announced, the Soviet Communist apparatus then taking the lead as it is now endeavoring to do in Latin America. Moderates, believing in liberty as well as in drastic reform, will come in for abuse—and worse. Each wing of extremists will circulate all manner of accusation against the statesmen and the parties of the center. Official and public opinion in the United States will have to be on guard against organized slander aimed at eliminating inconvenient individuals. It will also have to be on guard against overestimating occasional outbreaks of organized mob violence. Much of this violent talk and action is quite unrepresentative, minimal in terms of popular support, but maximal as noise-making propaganda and as embarrassment to local governments and their armies and police, who have a natural aversion to using force against any fraction of their own people.

As always in Latin America, the first line of conflict is among the "intellectuals." As it develops, the Alliance for Progress campaign should not be, and probably will not be, primarily a clash between the United States and the Communist powers. It should be a clash between the "free world" and its opponents, the imperialist left. The "free world" may be and probably is a political euphemism. Morally, however, it is a vast and tough reality. In defending liberal democracy and evolutionary change, the American position is effectively the same as that of the currently dominant influences in Western Europe. It is to be hoped that European thought, notably French, British, and Italian, will make itself felt. Intellectuals of European formation understand the conflict better than most Americans. They have been through it before. Those Latin American universities still free to act and student organizations, many of which are as passionately devoted to the liberal point of view as their rivals are committed to the Communist imperial cause, offer groups of dedicated adherents and training grounds for men who will be effective in society on behalf of political freedom and economic progress.

There will be debates in the press. The platform of the Alliance for Progress was well stated at the Montevideo Conference in August of 1961, following President Kennedy's outline of its purpose before the ambassadors of the American states at Washington on March 13, 1961. It is to be hoped, and the writer believes it can be arranged, that the primary debate will not be the conflict with overseas Communist imperialists. That conflict is, to be sure, an obstacle which must be overcome. But the main subject of the discussion is how governmental machinery, non-governmental machinery, publicly owned enterprise, privately owned business, and all elements in the population, high and humble, can best work toward bringing Latin America, economically and socially, into a modern world of productiveness with social justice.

The Latin American political parties of the center, ranging in complexion from moderate socialist to moderate conservative but all agreeing on the absolute necessity of maintaining freedom and opportunity for the individual, can and should form a working alliance. Steps toward this cooperation have already been taken. These parties in the various countries have been in touch with each other, through informal meetings at San José, Costa Rica, and at Lima. Slowly there is coming into existence an inter-American democratic internationale, whose combined strength represents more than a majority of all votes cast in Latin American elections. A parallel and allied force already flourishing is the Inter-American Press Association.

Until the holding of the two Punta del Este conferences these parties and groups and intellectuals had no defined political objective. The Alliance for Progress provides it. As in Europe, after the Soviet walk-out from the Paris conference to discuss the Marshall Plan, the direct political issue was whether a country would be for and would implement, or was against and would reject, the Marshall Plan. This is now the specific issue in Latin America—and should continue to be the issue.

The Cuban affair is thus placed in context. Its importance is plain enough—but what happens to Cuba is, clearly, secondary to what happens in the hemisphere as a whole. Immediately, Cuba is dangerous because her imperial Communist captors intend and propose to prevent the other American countries from peacefully determining their own destiny. They intend, using Cuba as agent and arsenal, to impose solutions designed by and in the interest of Moscow or Peiping. Blocking this attack is primarily important because only then can the Latin American countries determine their own solution. That solution transcends the Cuban question.

Throughout the entire Latin American area most political

groups outside the reactionary right are determined to break out of the stalemate which has held great areas in social, economic, and intellectual stagnation. They have already achieved far more than most North Americans appreciate. Cities like Buenos Aires and Mendoza, São Paulo and Brasilia, Bogotá and Caracas, or San José in Costa Rica are not the product of stagnation. The difficulty is that the cities are too often vigorously developing islands surrounded by areas not yet touched with capacity to progress.

The prospects of success in the campaign under way are good for the free world. This does not mean that the campaign will be easy, or soon over, or that there will not be dangerous and painful moments in it. Nevertheless, analysis of the elements involved seem to justify a sober optimism.

Critical Areas

Mention must be made of certain stormy areas. It is invidious to note, but absurd to ignore, existence of points of possible stress. These are the primary targets in the campaign of the overseas Communist powers.

Prime on their target list is Venezuela. It makes no difference that the present Venezuelan government is democratic, has a solid popular mandate, has achieved notable progress in social reorganization, or that its agrarian reform law is in operation and is working steadily, or that its educational system already provides facilities for every child of primary-school age. It has struggled manfully and on the whole successfully to clean up the legacy of gigantic problems left it by the Pérez Jiménez dictatorship. It has evolved a viable and rapidly progressing industrial development in the Caroni area. Because of the large foreign investment in the country's oil fields and the resulting economic importance of Venezuela, overseas Communist strategy is aimed at capturing the country; and Cuban Communist tactics will continue to be directed against it. For practical purposes their hard-core cadres are effective chiefly in the city of Caracas and one or two smaller centers; they are a tiny minority. They are in part armed now, but the growing fleet of fast small craft accumulated by Castro is undoubtedly aimed at setting up a supply line by sea.

Castro, indeed, tried to seize Venezuela by a coup in Caracas during the Punta del Este Conference of January 1962. His failure indicated Communist weakness, but we must assume nevertheless that Venezuela will need continuing support. The program of control of Cuban arms voted at Punta del Este will have particular usefulness in this area.

Parts of Colombia are likely to be foci of trouble. For decades certain rural areas and even cities have remained outside the effective scope of the authority of the Colombian government at Bogotá. These are sometimes called "bandit cities," held by guerrillas who are gangsters and *insurrectos* rather than Communists. But they offer tempting opportunity for Communist operations of the Chinese variety, directed against Bogotá. Directly east of the Panamanian border there are valleys with access to the sea connecting with areas much of which have never accepted any central Colombian authority. From there a clandestine corridor into Ecuador is readily possible, perhaps already has been established.

The Colombian army is only just beginning to solve the practical problem presented by Communist or independent guerrillas in the mountain areas. Meanwhile, in Bogotá itself, the statesmanlike agreement negotiated by President Lleras Camargo and Conservative leaders, designed to maintain the country's unity and basic cooperation between the two parties, Liberal and Conservative, during the transition away from the Rojas Pinilla dictatorship, is under attack. The structure of cooperation will be under inevitable strain in 1962, a year of election and transfer of the presidential office to a Conservative.

The adjacent state of Ecuador is probably the scene of intensive Communist-imperialist operations now, activities not readily apparent in the capital at Quito. The attempt will be made—perhaps is already being made—to place Communists or their allies in strategically located police headquarters, in minor but powerful positions in the Departments of Interior and Police and of Education, and in key posts in the army. Behind these would be secret centers, probably in the Ecuadoran lowland, from which the hard-core cadres can eventually launch guerrilla operations. Combined Communist operations in Colombia and Ecuador could conceivably precipitate a variety of Spanish civil war whose chief foreseeable outcome would be a ghastly debris of corpses, suffering, and devastation.

Central America, and more particularly Guatemala, presents another probable area for Communist attack. In part, the motivation here is sentimental. In the early 1950s Communist-imperialist organization headed by an Argentine, Ernesto (Che) Guevara, almost achieved supremacy in Guatemala under the presidency of the pro-Communist Jacobo Arbenz. The regime was overthrown when Arbenz undertook to import arms from the Communist bloc (the only possible use of which could have been to attack the adjacent countries in Central America), anti-Communist forces raised the standard of revolt, and neither army nor people rallied to the support of Arbenz. Guevara took refuge in Mexico, thereafter joined Castro, and has been one of the chief organizers of the Communist regime in Cuba. He and the other Communist associates who failed in Guatemala have never forgiven nor forgotten their failure and intend to retrieve it.

President Ydígoras Fuentes, a capable political leader, understands this threat perfectly. He intends that Guatemala shall be defended. He also has displayed remarkable ability in pushing through the Guatemalan congress a number of basic measures of social reform—for example, a graduated income tax and the outline of a program for land reform and for housing. But Guatemala, nearly half of which is composed of Mayan Indians, has to cope with a composite racial and social structure, and with the results of long neglect of her social, educational, and economic problems under previous governments. She still bears the scars of the abortive class war launched by Guevara and Arbenz. The government and people need above all a period free of uproar and violence, so that the real purpose of the Alliance for Progress—raising productivity, distributing national product more equitably and effectively, and organizing the country for greater economic and social progress—may go forward.

Finally, an "x" factor. British Guiana (about to become independent under the name of "Eldorado") may undertake to play a role in the affairs of the continent and the Caribbean Sea. A majority of her population is oriental—chiefly Indian. Only a fraction of it is Hispanic. The immediately dominant figure in the emerging state, Cheddi Jagan, is Hindu; he has little appeal to the nonoriental population, and even within the oriental majority he is opposed by a small but active Muslim group. He has consistently favored Castro, which suggests an undisclosed alliance with, if not his own membership in, the Communist network. (It is a standard Leninist tactic at this stage not to disclose such membership; but Jagan's real orientation toward—or away from— overseas Communist imperialism should be determinable in the near future.)

The incoming state, not hitherto a member of the American system, introduces a problem the hemisphere has not yet had to face. One possibility can be foreseen. At one time, in pursuit of the expansionist policies of an earlier age, the British on behalf of Guiana claimed Venezuelan territory up to the lower southeastern bank of the Orinoco River. This would include a notable part of the area now under development by Venezuela. Venezuela on her side has counterclaims. If Cheddi Jagan were to follow the policy of President Sukarno of Indonesia in claiming everything ever claimed by the European parent country when the area was a colony (while, of course, bitterly denying the legitimacy of past imperialism), dangerous and unpleasant issues might be forced. It seems likely that any such action would immediately excite apprehension and opposition from all the neighboring Latin American states, irrespective of any other consideration. Under former President Quadros, for example, Brazil seriously considered at one time the sending of contingents of the Brazilian army into British Guiana.

The Caribbean archipelago will for some period of time be an area of tension. The Dominican Republic has still to repair the great cost in human resources and in organizational power occasioned by the long dictatorship of the late Generalissimo Rafael Trujillo. There is reason to believe the Dominican people will successfully resolve that problem. Manifestly, the Castro regime in Cuba will create as much trouble as it can. It made no secret of its intent to seize the Dominican government in the disorganization following the dictator's assassination; it has small but active cadres there now.

On the other end of the island of Hispaniola lies the painfully overpopulated misgoverned republic of Haiti, solidly Negro with a mulatto upper crust. With standards of living, of education and government perhaps the lowest in the hemisphere, it inevitably attracts Communist attention and activity.

It is a standard tactic of overseas Communist propagandists to present Puerto Rico as a "colony" held (according to them) against its will by the brutal imperialism of the United States. This fantastically mendacious myth is, of course, as contrary to the facts as anything could be. Puerto Rico's status was freely determined by a plebiscite of Puerto Ricans who chose by an overwhelming majority to be a free state within the defense and economic system of the United States because this was far and away the most advantageous arrangement they could make or achieve. There is opposition—but the opposition desires to be annexed to the United States as a state. Communist propaganda against Puerto Rico masquerades under the slogan of "Independence." In the two and one-half million Puerto Ricans they have been able to muster not more than two or three hundred individuals. One cannot on that count keep the propaganda of Moscow and Peiping (which is actually not more intelligent than any other kind of propaganda) from insisting on claims which, however stupid, may attract attention or adherence in other countries. The companion tactic—to foment occasional assassination plots—has been tried and has failed.

The Task Ahead

Defensively, the democratic forces in the hemisphere and with them the United States may have their hands full in the next two or three years. The writer believes, nevertheless, that the zenith of Communist effort and success has been reached, and may perhaps have already passed. Or, at any rate, that their climactic effort is not far away and will come at a time when it can be decisively met and defeated.

This is one of the results of the January 1962 conference at

Punta del Este. That conference forced the issue. Had it been delayed, the struggle might have been brought to climax after, rather than before, Communist preparations were complete. In diplomacy, as in war, strategy consists in compelling the opponent to fight at a time and place and in circumstances chosen by the strategist. The cold war undeniably compels some diversion of effort from the main purpose of the Alliance for Progress, but it is unavoidable. As matters stand, the need for defense need not seriously prejudice or indeed unduly impede the main, positive campaign; indeed, the Alliance for Progress effort should itself be a notable part of the defense of the hemisphere in the broad sense of that concept.

Meanwhile a great deal of constructive work will go forward, both in economic progess and in social development. The fact of unrest, presently fomented by overseas Communist powers, is not likely to prevent the growth of crops, the extension of manufacturing facilities, or the increase of Latin American productivity at or about an average rate of 4 or 5 per cent per year. In a substantial number of countries, and these the largest, economic processes have a way of continuing, even under cover of a considerable amount of political noise. Meanwhile, a good many governments are seriously attacking the problem of assuring better distribution of income through programs of land and taxation reform and in some cases through vigorous educational effort. The public-sector infrastructure of roads, transport, and sanitation shows visible progress.

If the Alliance for Progress is vigorously pushed and well handled, it will provide an effective outlet for the energy and idealism of the younger men in Latin America. A number of these younger men come from the group loosely classified by American journalists as "the oligarchy," though more are drawn from the relatively new "middle class." Both descriptions belie their motives and their approach. Most of them have few illusions about maintaining the *status quo,* and in most cases their motives transcend purely personal calculations of advantage.

To these men, the real enemy is not a Communist agitator—he is an obstacle, of course, but by no means the main issue. The real enemy is stagnation in poverty, undersupply in the presence of the technical possibility of sufficiency, ignorance where education is possible. This is a youth element which scarcely existed in Russia at the time of the revolution of 1917, and which would have revolutionized Cuba had it not been betrayed into a dictatorship supported by Russian arms. Latin American governments in most instances will be cooperative, whatever their reasons. The task is challenging and is enormous. But it can be achieved. We have outlined in these pages the immediate difficulties because they intrude themselves upon the scene. They must not be allowed to obscure either the resources or capacity or the quietly moving current of economic and social achievement. Only as one contrasts the condition of most Latin American countries today with those prevailing ten or twenty years ago does the fact of progress become striking—as the fact of its absence is striking in a few countries which must command our sympathy and attention.

2. Outline of the Future

American policy can be soundly based only if it is informed by a realistic estimate of conditions which will obtain in the farther future—say, twenty-five years from now. In any attempt to sketch the outline of such a picture the margin of error is undeniably great. Yet, in making it, realism and necessity as well as observable trends of ideas give some guide. Irrespective of the cold war, irrespective of space exploration and intercontinental missiles, most of the fundamentals of life in this hemisphere have not changed and will not change. The Latin American area will be populated by more than three hundred millions of people. They will be living on the ground; they will need food, shelter, and occupations; they will seek them at a standard and level giving immediate satisfaction. Their intellectual life will continue in the language they understand; they will live in a social framework, however changed by evolution or revolution, which will nevertheless continue to approximate the habits of previous generations. The hemisphere will continue to be separated from the old world by two great oceans, despite the fact that these will be swiftly and easily crossed. The aggregate of economic and social necessities and the momentum of race and cultural habits will continue to be greater in volume and force than the political ideas prevalent in any one of the national units which will then make up Latin America. The material and physical organization of agriculture and industry and the welding of society by land, sea, and air will reflect this aggregate necessity—perhaps, more accurately, this aggregate of wants and habits.

Current stresses and strains in Latin America essentially reflect the liquidation of outworn social organization. This was in effect the hold-over framework and body of political and social habits remaining after the colonial empires were ended in early nineteenth century. Liquidation of empire did not liquidate social form. Some of this organization, some of these habits, are not adaptable to the later twentieth century. Some of them are adaptable and will be and should be preserved. In the United States it is not generally appreciated, for example, that the Spanish imperial colonial code (the Laws of the Indies), though honored in the breach as well as in much of the observance, was the most enlightened colonial code of its time; in some respects, perhaps, it was the most successful colonial code in the world. Some of its political protections—one thinks of the institution of the "residency" as a curb on the absolute power of colonial governors—are in effect in parts of Latin America today.

Diversity and Unity

One element stands out in determining the horizon and the pattern of the generation hence: the development of a degree of unity. This unity will be real, whereas up to now Latin American solidarity, like the inter-American system, has been an intellectual conception rather than an integral fact. The reason is that the elements of unity now present will increasingly be emphasized by elements of necessity. Taken together, they should overmaster the diversities in the region. One hopes elements of a diversity will be preserved—the culture would be infinitely less rich without them—but they are likely to survive only in a common protection frame.

Regional unification will not avoid stresses and strains, and to the coming generation these strains are likely to appear formidable. Brazil will have grown to the status of a "great power" of second rank, with greater possibilities ahead. She will, as she always has, blow hot and cold on the subject of regional unity. She may even experiment with local imperialism, though this is not in the Brazilian tradition. But her vast territory, her growing population, her preoccupation with her own great plains and the continuing struggle with the Amazon jungle, as population pressure compels her toward it, will at that period turn her more to continental isolationism than to conquest, more toward concentration on regional matters than toward world politics. Her common frontier with all but two South American states, as well as her own tolerant and absorptive intellectual formation, suggests that she will continue the great tradition of Baron Rio Branco, who successfully settled Brazilian problems by law rather than force. Economically, though more nearly capable of self-sufficiency than other Latin American states, she will nevertheless need them—as they will need her.

The South American states will increasingly work together. Probably the next generation will see the emergence on the Andean plateau of a powerful Indian movement coloring and adding richness to the picture. That development will still be in infancy; proper handling of it, indeed, will be one of the great problems for Latin American statesmen of the future.

The Caribbean states—those of the Antillean archipelago and of the mainland surrounding the sea—will have developed a powerful common interest. They will constitute a subregion. It will be more than a mere Mediterranean community, because its industrial and energy potential will be enormous, like that of the Ruhr basin in Europe.

Mexico will be less uneasily aloof. Her development will have precipitated her into that contact both with the United States and with other neighboring countries which up to now has been present only in limited degree. Her Amerindian culture will have become self-assured, will have attained world recognition as an element powerfully enriching the art of the world.

Despite its diverse elements, the necessities and pressures of population, trade, economics, the common currency of language and intellectual habit, join in dictating a growing integration for the whole of Latin America. At the opening of this study we noted that the transport, communication, and contact giving reality to the intellectual conception of unity only began at the close of World War II. Their cumulative effect and multiplication will have become powerful twenty-five years from now; the region in that respect may be almost as closely knit as is the United States today.

This developing unity of Latin America should be in harmony with the United States, if indeed the United States is not an integral part of it. The writer hopes for the latter solution—not because it will add to U.S. power but because it will add to the stability, the productiveness and the defense of a region whose existence may well be threatened at that time from the Asian continent.

This harmony is not a foregone conclusion. Yet the balance of probability suggests it. Parts of Latin America may, as has Cuba, become provinces of old world Communist empires. That phase will be short. Communist colonies are as vulnerable as any other colonies. Further, to serious observers it is apparent that the Communist imperial system is already obsolete economically as well as politically. Its directing dogmatism prevents its evolution. In any case, the social solution chosen by any Latin American people will not imply permanent subservience to overseas imperialism, though liberation from it would be a long and bloody road. One remembers the eagerness with which most of Latin America adopted the ideas of the French Revolution—and the swift resistance that promptly developed when, in the name of that revolution, agents and armies of Napoleon appeared in the Western Hemisphere. The Russian Revolution is now in its Napoleonic phase—it now depends on its guns; it is, internationally, a power system rather than a social revolution; it immediately becomes hostile even to elements practicing its Communist ideas and methods which refuse obedience to its power.

The relation of the United States to the region could take either of two forms: harmonious and cooperative friendship between the United States and a separate but more or less integrated Latin American group, or a degree of integration of the

United States in that group. At the moment, the former tendency is suggested by current political events but is being denied by deeper necessities of economics and defense, which suggest integration rather than mere "good relations." There is pathos in the cry of some Latin American leaders that, politically, they must be somehow "liberated" from the United States, while at the same time they take for granted inter-American economic cooperation and assume favorable stabilization of markets and economic assistance from the United States in a manner and on a scale unknown between independent countries in previous history.

A great barrier to integration in a hemispheric regional system lies in the United States itself. Here a quite different orientation is being urged, with power, by intellectual and journalistic as well as political elements. These people do not take, and never have taken, Latin America very seriously; most of them do not know the region at all. To them, the wave of the future is the "Atlantic Community," by which they mean integration of the United States into a common economic-cultural-military complex with Britain and Western Europe. They, like many Latin Americans who look to Europe alone, have yet to envisage the possibility that the United States may be in both complexes. In the long view it may become possible, as Bolívar dreamed, to combine the two systems in a larger Atlantic community. These are problems that lie ahead. Quite likely they will be facing the governments of both worlds in the future period we are imagining.

To this writer the main question is not whether there will be an inter-American system. There will be. The question is how perilous and bloody the road may become if attempt is made to discard it and to Balkanize the region, forcing the constituent countries to re-establish by any means possible the peaceful framework on which their peoples must increasingly depend.

Policies for the Future

In determining their policies for the future the United States and the Latin American nations must both pay heed to three main strands of the growing fabric of unity.

First, viable regional political organization will have been established conforming to the actual unity of the region. Initially it should take the form of coordination of action among the Latin American states and with the United States, similar to the coordination coming into existence in Europe now. In the long pull, coordination may become actual political union in some form of federation or confederation, toward which Western Europe is already groping. It seems improbable that Latin America will have reached the phase of imminent union in twenty-five years. But it will have—indeed it will have to have—a working political coordination which it clearly does not have today.

The Organization of American States, and its companion mechanisms, will have been reorganized. Reorganization may arise out of failure of the current institutions. But if they are liquidated, equivalent institutions will have to be reinvented. Reorganization may come less spectacularly, by revising and doing better the work attempted at Bogotá in 1948. There need be neither recrimination nor regret when this happens. The Organization of American States under the Charter of Bogotá replaced an agreement for common consultation worked out by President Roosevelt, Sumner Welles, and the writer, and accepted by Latin America, at Buenos Aires in 1936. The Bogotá Charter perhaps assumed a degree of unity and capacity to reach a consensus greater than that which really existed. At present, the hemispheric organization is in effect reverting to the practice of "consultation."

As time goes on, a growing degree of political integration is almost dictated by necessity where a large number of national states is concerned. Rationalization, coordination, harmonization are actually the only alternatives to unification by federation or empire. The United States does not desire empire for herself. Nor will she tolerate empire in Latin America if attempted by any overseas power—as attempts have been made in the past, are being made now, and will be made in the future.

Second, economic development will be an impelling force toward a unified region. Through the mechanism of the Alliance for Progress the American community of nations announces its intention of moving toward recognition that the unity of the hemisphere rests on development of a common and effective economic organization. In practical economics, after all, integration is really taking place day by day.

The sketch picture suggests that twenty-five years hence Latin America will have a common market. At that time her already substantial capacity for production, including all manner of industrialization, will have approached the degree of industrialization the United States had in 1939—perhaps, the degree of industrialization the United States has today. The region will have come closer to "catching up" with the United States. It will have multiplied many times the present trickle of trade between the countries. Latin America will not be able to attain this goal, however, or manage it if attained, if the economic policy of the region is split into twenty-one warring units. This the governments and their peoples already recognize, intellectually if not emotionally. In one form or another the common market will have been organized, will have become so basic to regional economic operation that few Latin American countries would, and perhaps could, effectively break it.

A common banking, currency and credit system will have been achieved. This seems beyond political possibility today. But not farther beyond political possibilities than it seemed in Europe when the early plan for an integrated European economy was first developed in Washington in the year 1944. The effort should not be made now, save on the most limited scale. But, twenty-five years hence, something like this will probably have been done, will indeed have become essential. Probably it will have been achieved in institutional forms unknown now, as, for example, the jointly stabilized currencies in Europe are essential to the success of their common market. This involves sacrifices of "sovereignty" in certain respects—notably, sacrifice of the sovereign right to depreciate currency. But, as in the case of all such sacrifices, it would be made because (and only because) countervailing advantage gave greater freedom for exercise of sovereignty. As of today, use of this sovereign privilege amounts, in fact, to cutting a country off from contact with other countries who have elected not to follow inflation as a means of distributing wealth, levying taxation, and temporarily avoiding unpleasant political and social issues.

At that time, too, predominance of industrial employment over agriculture will have been definitely achieved. Whereas today some 70 per cent of Latin Americans are employed in a relatively inefficient agriculture, then 70 per cent will probably be employed in industry, distribution and other nonagricultural occupations. The methods of agriculture will so change that, indeed, there will be more men on the farms than is indicated by the need for their products. The movement of people from countryside to cities will become a flood, requiring drastic measures in the field of social policy to keep pace with economic change. Some at least of the growing pains of industry will have been surmounted. By that time there will be tools in existence which we are only barely beginning to understand now. These tools will be not only mechanical and technical, but economic and social as well. For one thing, the value created by a growing industry—which in the United States takes the form of several hundred billions of dollars of value assigned to the stock of corporations—can be guided and distributed where it is most needed for material and cultural development. Thus, a social tool which the United States did not have when she created her own industrial system will be available to Latin American economists and statesmen.

Finally, a system of inter-American transport will have been worked out, whereas today it exists only in suggestive outline. Road and truck transport from almost anywhere to anywhere else it is needed will have become readily possible in Latin America, as it now is in the United States. Air transport presumably will have been developed; here, Latin America keeps roughly equal in technique if not in density with developments elsewhere in the Western world. Probably local transport problems then will still reflect a congeries of local difficulties; but the great trunk routes and main feeder lines on land, sea, and air will have come into existence.

The economic forecast is thus by no means a pessimistic one. But, as in present-day Europe, all these developments can have their full significance only within a coordinated market economy, and under conditions of political order.

The Latin American region is likely to exhibit a diversity of social systems. They will probably include socialism in one or another form, as well as remnants of European-style capitalism, but predominantly they will be based on the mixed system prevailing in the United States. In certain parts, notably the Indian regions, norms of proprietorship unknown to us may appear. (In some substantial Indian race groups, "private" property is considered unworthy of a man's attention; it is therefore left almost exclusively to women and children.) Assignment of ownership in production which is not and cannot be a matter of personal possession and craft skill is a complex affair. Attaining the proper "mix" of private property and administrative power to obtain the greatest efficiency in production and distribution requires great sophistication. Unquestionably the Alliance for Progress will have to deal with, and may assist in, the development of forms as yet unknown to the United States.

Third, there is an impelling elemental nexus making for regional unity consisting of a common core of intellectual and cultural conceptions, powerfully reinforced by the common communication of the Spanish and Portuguese languages.

Latin America derived from its three centuries of Iberian imperial domination a single dominant religion—the Roman Catholic; a single dominant system of law—the Roman Law and Spanish Codes (now beginning to be modified); and an overriding framework of cultural and esthetic norms. These three currents are strong not only in and of themselves but because of the habits they create. The most violent of revolutions, as we have come to learn, does not change folk habits in these respects. More often it intensifies them and translates them into different idioms, or directs them toward different subjects of concern.

The Catholic religion prevails in most of the area. Its current, unhappily, has been sluggish and weak during the past century; it is only becoming aware of itself now. Inexplicably, the Vatican and the Catholic hierarchy virtually ceased to pay real attention to the Latin American region after its liberation from empire a century and a half ago. This is a surprising fact, because for the past forty years Latin America has embodied the largest choate Catholic constituency in the world. It is idle here to speculate on the reasons for this neglect. It is more significant to note that, in the past few years, there have been signs of a substantial renaissance in Catholic attitudes, energy, and drive. Many of the most constructive experiments and most useful activities in the region are now being carried forward through Catholic impetus and not infrequently under the direct leadership of Catholic priests. It would be merely frivolous not to recognize that the Catholic religion and the Catholic Church form one of the great emotional common denominators of the region from the Rio Grande to the Strait of Magellan.

In possibility, Catholic organization offers the greatest single base for popular education and formation of cultural structure. Just as its disuse leads to regret over the loss of a mighty opportunity, its continued existence, taken together with the recent renaissance, suggests that the opportunity will be used in the next generation as it was missed in the last. When one sees the amazing results accomplished by a handful of dedicated priests— you may find them over the the crest of the Andes, in the debased regions on the coasts, in the slums of cities and in the pathetically neglected rural areas—one can gain some appreciation of the possibility. When, as now, many elements in the Catholic Church are prepared to tackle social questions with the same vigor with which it formerly attacked problems of language, theology, and colonization, conviction grows that the Catholic Church is almost certain to be a solid component of the slowly integrating region.

The Roman law is not less forceful. A Latin American lawyer transported from Mexico City to Buenos Aires may have temporary difficulty in adjusting to different procedures. But the conceptions with which he is dealing, the methods by which disputes are settled, and the general rules of conduct are the same. On its road away from Rome, Spanish law became flexible in absorbing and modifying institutions and social methods derived from non-Latin civilizations. Spanish law of property includes, for example, conceptions and institutions of community ownership unknown to English or American law. There is no reason to believe that the Latin American peoples would, or indeed could or should discard this common component of their life. It is possible to imagine them discarding a great many of their lawyers. Since the days of the Spanish conquest, Latin America has frequently taken a dim view of their positive contribution. Perhaps that is the fate of lawyers everywhere; it has been especially pronounced in many Latin countries. But there has not, thus far, been any desire to discard the general framework of Roman law.

An added unifying force is a general agreement on norms of literacy and artistic composition. Culturally, achievements in any Latin American country are current throughout the entire region. A good poem in Costa Rica is saluted in Santiago, Chile. A literary composition of merit in the Spanish language finds appreciation everywhere in the Spanish-speaking world and is not excluded indeed from Brazil. The famous Colombian "Book Fair" which takes place annually in Bogotá exhibits for admiration and sale the literary product of the entire Latin American region. Nor is it an accident that the Western Hemisphere's best known composer in our time was a Brazilian, the late Heitor Villa-Lobos. Writers and journalists move with relative ease from urban centers in one country to those of another. An intellectual from Uruguay or Mexico has his following, great or small, in many other countries as well.

As the new communications net is strengthened, as radio communication becomes more dense, as the circulation of periodicals increases, the common currency of language and thought is bound to expand. If the vast problem of education is brought under even partial control, the interchangeability of teachers and scholars will grow with it. Already, indeed, it is substantial. As there is in Latin America a reverence for the intellectual and the scholar almost equal to the reverence paid by Chinese in an older era, there is at least reason to believe that an intellectual infrastructure is growing both in depth and strength.

With all of these currents the United States, it is a pleasure to note, has growing relations, which for the most part are, and should be, extra-governmental. Relationships between the Catholic hierarchies in Latin America and those of the United States have been steadily strengthened during the past few years. American foundations have increasingly sought to cooperate with Latin American institutions of education and learning. As might be expected, these relations have been most successful in scientific fields, and especially in medicine where the vast experience of the Rockefeller Foundation affords an admirable base. They are being broadened into other fields. At least a beginning has been made in contacts between lawyers and law schools, so that lawyers in the United States and in Latin America understand the mental processes and procedures of their colleagues.

*   *   *

Surveying the whole scene, the prognosis is soberly optimistic. Some years ago, in a brilliant address at Strasbourg, the head of the Institute of Higher International Studies in Geneva, Jacques Freymond, hazarded a forecast. The world was then polarized between the West, centering on the United States, and the Communist world, centering on Moscow. The next phase, he thought, would be the progressive disintegration of both polarized groups. Stresses, strains, and political movements in the West European and North American societies would impair the unity of action of the Western nations, but there would also be a breakup in the unity of the Communist world. Events have proved him right. The fission in the Communist world is plainly visible. Strain on Western unity is clear enough though the West, with its greater ability to tolerate diversity without sacrificing its basic unity, is not subject to the political-ideological breaks and scissions that have begun to rend the Communist bloc.

The current decline of the inter-American system is a phenomenon similar to the decline of unity among the NATO nations. But the phase of disintegration is not likely to be permanent either. Particularly in Latin America, and between Latin America and the United States, the elements of common interest are far greater than the elements of opposed or contradictory interest. These are slowly affirming themselves. In their affirmation lies hope for the future. As usual in international affairs, the problem lies in inducing the holders of power in each country to recognize the obvious.

Index